The Grateful Servant by James Shirley

A COMEDIE.

As it was Presented with good Applause in the private House in Drury-Lane by Her Majesties Servants.

James Shirley was born in London in September 1596.

His education was through a collection of England's finest establishments: Merchant Taylors' School, London, St John's College, Oxford, and St Catharine's College, Cambridge, where he took his B.A. degree in approximately 1618.

He first published in 1618, a poem entitled Echo, or the Unfortunate Lovers.

As with many artists of this period full details of his life and career are not recorded. Sources say that after graduating he became "a minister of God's word in or near St Albans." A conversion to the Catholic faith enabled him to become master of St Albans School from 1623–25.

He wrote his first play, Love Tricks, or the School of Complement, which was licensed on February 10th, 1625. From the given date it would seem he wrote this whilst at St Albans but, after its production, he moved to London and to live in Gray's Inn.

For the next two decades, he would write prolifically and with great quality, across a spectrum of thirty plays; through tragedies and comedies to tragicomedies as well as several books of poetry. Unfortunately, his talents were left to wither when Parliament passed the Puritan edict in 1642, forbidding all stage plays and closing the theatres.

Most of his early plays were performed by Queen Henrietta's Men, the acting company for which Shirley was engaged as house dramatist.

Shirley's sympathies lay with the King in battles with Parliament and he received marks of special favor from the Queen.

He made a bitter attack on William Prynne, who had attacked the stage in Histriomastix, and, when in 1634 a special masque was presented at Whitehall by the gentlemen of the Inns of Court as a practical reply to Prynne, Shirley wrote the text—The Triumph of Peace.

Shirley spent the years 1636 to 1640 in Ireland, under the patronage of the Earl of Kildare. Several of his plays were produced by his friend John Ogilby in Dublin in the first ever constructed Irish theatre; The Werburgh Street Theatre. During his years in Dublin he wrote The Doubtful Heir, The Royal Master, The Constant Maid, and St. Patrick for Ireland.

In his absence from London, Queen Henrietta's Men sold off a dozen of his plays to the stationers, who naturally, enough published them. When Shirley returned to London in 1640, he finished with the Queen Henrietta's company and his final plays in London were acted by the King's Men.

On the outbreak of the English Civil War Shirley served with the Earl of Newcastle. However when the King's fortunes began to decline he returned to London. There his friend Thomas Stanley gave him help and thereafter Shirley supported himself in the main by teaching and publishing some educational works under the Commonwealth. In addition to these he published during the period of dramatic eclipse four small volumes of poems and plays, in 1646, 1653, 1655, and 1659.

It is said that he was "a drudge" for John Ogilby in his translations of Homer's Iliad and the Odyssey, and survived into the reign of Charles II, but, though some of his comedies were revived, his days as a playwright were over.

His death, at age seventy, along with that of his wife, in 1666, is described as one of fright and exposure due to the Great Fire of London which had raged through parts of London from September 2nd to the 5th.

He was buried at St Giles in the Fields on October 29th, 1666.

Index of Contents

To the Right Honourable, Francis Earl of Rutland, &c.

My most honoured Lord,

When the Age declineth from her primitive vertue, and the Silken wits of the Time, (that I may borrow from our acknowledg'd Master, learned JOHNSON) disgracing Nature, and harmonious Poesie, are transported with many illiterate and prodigious births, it is not safe to appear without protection. Among all the names of Honour, this Comedy oweth most gratitude to your Lordship, whose clear testimony to me was above a Theater, and I applaud the dexterity of my Fate, that hath so well prepared a Dedication, whither my only ambition would direct it. I am not pale, to think it is now expos'd to your deliberate censure; for 'tis my security, that I have studied your Lordships Candor, and know you imitate the Divine nature which is mercifull above offence. Go on great Lord, and be the volume of our English honour, in whom while others, invited by their birth, and quicknd with ambitious emulation, read and study their principles, let me be made happy enough to admire, and devote my self,

Your Lordships most humble creature
James Shirley

DRAMATIS PERSONAE

Duke of Savoy, Lover of Leonora; and in her supposed losse, of Cleona.
Lodwick, his Brother, wild and lascivious.
Foscari, a noble Count, and Lover of Cleona.
Grimundo, a Lord, and once Governor to Lodwick.
Noble men of Savoy.
Soranzo.
Giotto.
Fabrichio.
Piero, Companion of Lodwick.
Jacomo, a foolish ambitious Steward to Cleona.
Valentio, a religious man.
Abbot.
Gentleman.
Servants.
Satyrs.
Leonora, the Princess of Millan, but disguiz'd as a Page to Foscari, and call'd Dulcino.
Astella, a vertuous Lady, Wife to Lodwick, but neglected.
Belinda, Wife to Grimundo.
Cleona, Foscari's Mistris.
Ladies.
Nymphs.

THE SCENE - SAVOY

ACTUS I

SCENE I

A Room in the Duke's Palace.

Enter **SORANZO, GIOTTO.**

GIOTTO
The Duke is mov'd.

SORANZO
The newes displeas'd him much.

GIOTTO
And yet I see no reason why he should engage so great affection to th' Daughter
Of Millan; he nere saw her.

SORANZO
Fame doth paint
Great beauties, and her picture (by which Princes
Court one another) may beget a flame
In him to raise this passion.

GIOTTO
Trust a pencill.
I like not that State-woing: see his Brother

[Enter **LODWICK.**

Has left him. Pray my Lord how is it with
His Highnesse?

LODWICK
Somewhat calmer, Love I think
Will kill neither of us: although I be
No Stoick, yet I thank my Starres I have
A power o'r my affection, if hee'le not
Tame his, let it melt him into Sonnets,
He will prove the more loving Prince to you.
Get in again, and make wise speeches to him,
There is Aristotles Ghost still with him,
My Philosophical Governour that was:
He wants but you two, and a paire of Spectacles,
To see what folly 'tis to love a woman
With that wicked resolution to marry her.

Though he be my elder Brother, and a Duke,
I ha more wit: when there's a death of women
I may turn fool, and place one of their Sexe
Neerer my heart: farewel, commend me to
My Brother, and the Council-Table.

[Exit

SORANZO
Still the same wild Prince, there needs no character
Where he is, to expresse him.

GIOTTO
He said truth;
I doubt there is no roome for one, whom he:
Should place in's heart, and honour.

SORANZO
His own Lady
All pity her misfortune, both were too
Unripe for Hymen, 'twas the old Dukes act,
And in such marriages hearts seldom meet
When they grow older.

GIOTTO
Wherefore would the Duke
Marry his young sonne first?

SORANZO
The walke of Princes,
To make provision betimes for them:
They can bequath small legacy, knowing th' heir
Carries both state and fortune for himself,
His fate's before him, here comes Grimundo!

[Enter **GRIMUNDO**.

GRIMUNDO
The Duke is recollected, where's the Prince?

SORANZO
Gone.
I would he were return'd once to himself.

GIOTTO
He has too soone forgot your precepts.

SORANZO

Your example might still be a Lecture,

GRIMUNDO
I did not deceive the old Dukes trust
While I had power to manage him,
He's now past my tuition, but to the Duke—
Is it not strange my Lord, that the young Lady
Of Millan, should be forc'd to marry now, with
Her Uncle?

GIOTTO
They're unequal.

SORANZO
'Tis unlawful,

GRIMUNDO
'Tis a trifle, reasons of State they urge
Against us, least their Dukedome by this match,
Be subject unto Savoy, for the scruple
Of Religion, they are in hope that
A Dispensation may be procur'd
To quit exceptions, and by this means
They shall preserve their Principality,
I'th name and blood, so reports Fabrichio
Whom the Duke imployed for treaty: how now?

[Enter a **GENTLEMAN**.

GENTLEMAN
The Duke calls for you my Lords.

GIOTTO
We attend, Ha! he is coming forth.

[Enter **DUKE** and **FABRICHIO**.

SORANZO
His looks are cheerful.

DUKE
Fabrichio?

FABRICHIO
My Lord.

DUKE
We will to Tennis.

FABRICHIO

What your Grace please.—

DUKE

Grimundo?
Because you take no pleasure in such pastimes,
Your contemplation may busie it self with that book.

[Gives him a miniature.

GRIMUNDO

Book my Lord! it is—

DUKE

Leonora's picture, a fair Table-book,
You may without offence to your young wife
Look on a picture.
Millan and we are parted, our breast weares
Again his natural temper, allow me pray
The excuse of common frailty, to be moved
At strangenesse of this newes.

GIOTTO

Your Highnesse said, You would to Tennis.

DUKE

And 'tis time enough,
We have the day before us: some Prince Grimundo
In such a case as this would have been angry,
Angry indeed, thrown of cold language, and
Call'd it a high, and loud affront, whose stirring
Imagination would have weakened Death,
And by a miserable warre, have taught
Repentance, to a paire of flourishing States,
Such things there have been?

SORANZO

But your grace is wise—

DUKE

Nay, do not flatter now, I do not Court
Your praise so much, I speak but what our stories
Mention, if they abuse not soft posterity:
I was not come to tell you, what my thoughts,
With a strong murmure prompt me too.

GRIMUNDO

We hope—

DUKE
Ye fear, and do not know me yet, my actions
Shall clear your jealousie, I'me reconcil'd
At home, and while I cherisht a peace here,
Abroad I must continue it, there are
More Ladies i'the world?

FABRICHIO
Most true my Lord.

DUKE
And as attractive great, and glorious women,
Are there not, Ha!

SORANZO
Plenty my Lord i'the world.

DUKE
I'the world, within the confines of our Dukedome
In Savoy, are there not?

GRIMUNDO
In Savoy too.
Many choise beauties, but your birth my Lord—

DUKE
Was but an honour purchas'd by another,
It might have been thy chance.

GRIMUNDO
My Father was—No Duke.

DUKE
'Twas not thy fault, nor ist my vertue,
That I was born when the fresh Sunne was rising,
So came with greater shadow into life,
Than thou or he.

GRIMUNDO
But royal Sir be pleas'd—

DUKE
No more, weare not ignorant, you may
Take away this distinction, and alledge
In your grave wisdoms, specious arguments,
For your alliance with some forraign Prince,

But we have weighed their promising circumstance,
And find it only a device, that may
Serve time, and some dark ends, a meer state trick,
To disguise hatred, and is empty of
Those benefits, it seems to bring along:
Give me a Lady born in my obedience,
Whose disposition, will not engage
A search into the nature of her Climate,
Or make a scrutiny into the Starres:
Whose language is mine own, and will not need
A smooth Interpreter, whose vertue is
Above all titles, though her birth or fortune,
Be a degree beneath us, such a Wife
Were worth a thousand far fetcht Brides, that have
More state, and lesse Devotion.

FABRICHIO
If your Highnesse—

DUKE
Come you shall know our purpose, in the last
We obay'd your directions, not without
Our free and firm allowance of the Lady
Whom wee'l forget, it will become our duties,
Follow us now, we have not been unthrifty
In our affections, and I must tell you
Here we are fixt to marry.

GRIMUNDO
We are subjects,
And shall solicit Heaven, you may finde one
Worthy your great acceptance.

DUKE
We are confident,
And to put off the cloud we walk in, know
We are resolv'd to place all love and honour
Upon Cleona. Nor is't a new affection, we but cherish
Some seeds, which heretofore her vertue had
Scattered upon our heart.

GRIMUNDO
We cannot be
Ambitious of a Lady, in your own
Dominion, to whom we shall more willingly
Prostrate our duties.

SORANZO

She's a Lady of
A flowing sweetnesse, and the living vertue
Of many noble Ancestors.

GIOTTO
In whom
Their fortunes meet, as their Prophetick souls
Had taught them thrifty providence, for this
Great honour you intend her.

DUKE
We are pleas'd,
And thank your general vote:
You then shall straight prepare our visit, bear our
Princely respects, and say we shall take pleasure
To be her Guests to day: nay lose no time,
We shall the sooner quit the memory
Of Leonoraes Image.

[Enter **LODWICK**.

SORANZO
The Prince your brother Sir?

DUKE
Withdraw, but be not at too much distance.

[They retire.

Lodwick.
Y'are welcome.

LODWICK
I shall know that by my successe, I want
A thousand Crowns, a thousand Crowns.

DUKE
For what?

LODWICK
Why will these foolish questions ne'e be left,
Is't not sufficient I would borrow em,
But you must still capitulate with me?
I would put em to that use they were ordain'd for;
You might have well have ask't me, when I meant
To pay you again.

DUKE

That to some other men
Might ha been necessary.

LODWICK
And you wo'not
Do that, I have another easie suit to you.

DUKE
What is't?

LODWICK
A thing of nothing; I wo'd intreat you
To part with this same transitory honour,
This trifle call'd a Dukedome, and retire
Like a good Christian Brother, into some
Religious house, it would be a great ease to you,
And comfort to your friends, especially
To me, that would not trouble you with the noise
Of money thus, and I could help it.

DUKE
'Tis a kind and honest motion, out of Charity,
Meere Charity, so I must needs accept it—Why?
Ile only marry, and get a boy, or two,
To govern this poor trifle, for I'me bound
In duty, to provide for my succession.

LODWICK
What do you make of me, cannot I serve?

DUKE
You that propound a benefit for my soul,
Wo'not neglect your own I know: wee'le both
Turn Fryers together?

LODWICK
And be lowsie?

DUKE
Any thing.

LODWICK
I shall not have a thousand Crowns?

DUKE
Thou shalt.

LODWICK

Then be a duke still; come, lets love, and be
Fine Princes: and thou hadst but two or three
Of my conditions, by this hand I wo'd not
Care and thou wert immortal, so I might
Live with thee, and enjoy this worlds felicity.

DUKE
T'hast put me in tune, how shals be very merry
Now in the instant?

LODWICK
Merry?

DUKE
Yes.

LODWICK
Merry indeed?

DUKE
Yes.

LODWICK
Follow me.
Ile bring you to a Lady.

DUKE
To a Whore.

LODWICK
That is a little the courser name.

DUKE
And can you play the Pander for me?

LODWICK
A toy, a toy.
What can a man do lesse for any brother?
Th'ordinary complement now a days, with great ones,
We prostitute our sisters with lesse scruple
Than eating flesh on vigils; 'tis out of fashion
To trust a servant with our private sins;
The greater tye of blood, the greater faith,
And therefore Parents have been held of late
The safest wheeles on which the childrens lust
Hath hurried into act, with supple greatnesse.
Nature doth wear a vertuous charm, and will
Do more in soft compassion to the sin,

Than gold or swelling promises.

DUKE
O Lodwick!
These things do carry horror, he is lost
I fear; no I ha thought of something else,
You shall with me to a Lady.

LODWICK
With all my heart.

DUKE
Unto my Mistresse.

LODWICK
Your Mistresse, who's that?

DUKE
The fair Cleona.

LODWICK
She is honest.

DUKE
Yes, were she otherwise, she were not worth my visit;
Not to lose circumstance, I love her.

LODWICK
How?

DUKE
Honestly.

LODWICK
You do not mean to marry her?

DUKE
It sha'not be my fault if she refuse
To be a Dutchesse.

LODWICK
A'my Conscience,
You are in earnest.

DUKE
As I hope to thrive in desires, come
You shall bear me company, and witnesse
How I woe her.

LODWICK
I commend
Your nimble resolution; then a Wise
Must be had somewhere, wo'd y'ad mine, to coole
Your appetite, take your own course, I can
But pray for you; the thousand Crowns—

DUKE
Upon condition, you'l not refuse, to Accompany.—

LODWICK
Your Caroach quickly—stay—
Now I think better on't, my Wife lives with her,
They are companions, I had forgot that?

DUKE
She'll take it kindly.

LODWICK
It were enough to put her
Into conceipt, I come in love to her;
My Constitution will not bear it.

DUKE
What? Not see her?

LODWICK
Yet a thousand Crowns—God buy
Condemne me to my wife.

[Exit.

[**GRIMUNDO** and the rest come forward.

DUKE
Ye hear Gentlemen?

GRIMUNDO
With grief my Lord, and wonder at your sufferance.

DUKE
He is our Brother, we are confident
Though he be wild he loves us, 'twill become
Us t' pray and leave him to a miracle,
But to our own affair.
Love and thy golden Arrow, we shall trie,
How you'll decide our second Destinie.

[Exeunt.

Foscari's Lodgings.

[Enter **FOSCARI** with a Letter.

FOSCARI
A kisse, and then 'tis sealed; this she would know
Better than the impression, which I made,
With the rude signet; 'tis the same she left
Upon my lip, when I departed from her,
And I have kept it warm still, with breath,
That in my prayers have mentioned her.

[Enter **DULCINO**.

DULCINO
My Lord?

FOSCARI
Dulcino welcome: Thou Art soon return'd.
How dost thou like the City?

DULCINO
'Tis a heap of handsome building.

FOSCARI
And how the people?

DULCINO
My conversation hath not age enough
To speak of them, more than they promise well
In their aspect: but I have argument
Enough in you, my Lord, to fortifie
Opinion, they are kind, and hospitable to Strangers.

FOSCARI
Thy indulgence to my wound,
Which owes a Cure unto thy pretty Surgery,
Hath made thee too much Prisoner to my chamber,
But we shall walk abroad.

DULCINO

It was my duty?
Since you receiv'd it in my cause; and could
My blood have wrought it sooner, it had been
Your balmy Fountain.

FOSCARI
Noble youth, I thank thee.

[Enter **SERVANT**.

How now, didst speak with him?

SERVANT
I had the happinesse, My Lord, to meet him
Waiting upon the Duke abroad: he bid me
Make haste with the remembrance of his Service:
He'll bring his own joys with him instantly,
To welcome your return.

FOSCARI
Didst thou reqnest
His secresie?

SERVANT
I did, he promis'd silence.

[Exit.

FOSCARI
So, I'le expect him, thou art sad Dulcino,
I prophesie thou shalt have cause, to bless
The minute, that first brought us to acquaintance.

DULCINO
Do not suspect my Lord, I am so wicked,
Not to do that already, you have saved
My life, and therefore have deserv'd that dutie.

FOSCARI
Name it no more, I mean another way.

DULCINO
It is not in your power, to make me Richer,
With anie benefit, shall succeed it, though
I should live ever with you.

FOSCARI
I require,

Not so much gratitude.

DULCINO
There is no way
Left for my hope, to do you any service,
Near my preserving, but by adding one
New favour, to a suit, which I would name.

FOSCARI
To me, I prethee speak, it must be something
I can deny thee.

DULCINO
'Tis an humble suit,
You license my departure.

FOSCARI
Whither?

DULCINO
Any whither.

FOSCARI
Do you call this a way to do me service?

DULCINO
It is the readiest I can studie Sir;
To tarrie were but to increase my debt,
And waste your favours; in my absence, I
May publish, how much vertue I have found
In Savoy, and make good unto your fame.
What I do owe you here, this shall survive you,
For I will speak the story with that truth,
And strength of passion, it shall do you honour,
And dwell upon your name sweeter than Myrrhe,
When we are both dead?

FOSCARI
Thou hast art, to move
In all things, but in this, change thy desire,
And I'le denie thee nothing; do not urge
Thy unkind departure, thou hast met perhaps,
With some that have deceiv'd thee with a promise,
Won with thy prettie looks and presence; but
Trust not a great man, most of them dissemble,
Pride, and Court-cunning hath betrai'd their faith,
To a secure Idolatry, their soul
Is lighter than a complement; take heed,

They'le flatter thy too young ambition,
Feed thee with names, and then like subtle Chimists
Having extracted, drawn thy spirit up,
Laugh, they have made thee miserable.

DULCINO
Let
No jealousie my Lord, render me so
Unhappie, that preferments or the flatteries
Of anie great man hath seduc'd my will
To leave you.

FOSCARI
Still I suspect thy safety?
And thou maist thus deceive me, it may be,
Some wanton Ladie hath beheld thy face,
And from her eyes shot Cupids into thine.
Trust not the innocence of thy soul too far,
For though their bosoms carrie whiteness, think,
It is not snow, they dwell in a hot Climate,
The Court, where men are but deceitful shadows,
The women, walking flames; what if this Ladie
Bestow a wealthie Carkanet upon thee,
Another give thee Wardrobes, a third promise
A Chain of Diamonds, to deck thy youth,
'Tis to buy thy vertue from thee, and when
Thy outside thrives, upon their treacherous bountie
Th' outstarve at heart, and lust will leave thy bodie
Manie unpitied Ruines, thou art young—

DULCINO
There is no fear my Lord, that I shall take
Such wicked courses, and I hope you see not
Anie propension in my youth, to sin
For pride, or wantonness.

FOSCARI
Indeed I do not,
But being my boy so young, and beautiful,
Thou art apt to be seduc'd.

DULCINO
Believe me Sir,
I will not serve the greatest Prince on earth
When I leave you.

FOSCARI
Thou shalt not serve me, I

Will make thee my companion.

DULCINO
No Reward,
Though just, should buy the freedom I was born with,
Much less base ends, if I but meet agen
That good man, who in Reverence to his habit,
The theeves let go before your happie valour
Came to my Rescue.

FOSCARI
He that was your Conduct
From Millan, for so—if I remember
You named a Father, what could he advantage
Your fortune, were he present, more, than with
Religious Counsel?

DULCINO
I did trust him Sir,
As being the safest treasurer, with that
Would make me welcom in Savoy, and
I know he will be faithful, when we meet.
For his sake let me beg you would discharge
A worthless Servant, that inquest of him—

FOSCARI
No more, to cut off all unwelcom motives,
I charge thee by thy Love, thy Gratitude,
Thy life preserv'd, which but to stay thee here,
I would not name agen; urge no consent
From me, to thy departure, I have now
Use of thy faith, thou wo't not run away;
I have employment for thee, such a one
As shall not onlie pay my services,
But leave me in arrerage to thy love.
Receive this letter.

[Enter **GRIMUNDO**.

Let me embrace thee with a spreading arm.

GRIMUNDO
I have dispens'd with my attendance on
The Duke, to bid you welcom Sir from death;
Fame so had couz'nd our belief, but thus
She has made you the more precious.

FOSCARI

Then I prospered,
If I may call it so, for I procur'd
That Rumour to be spread, excuse a minute,
I'le tell thee all my Counsels, I need not
Waste anie instructions on thee Dulcino,
For the conveyance of this paper, let me
Commend it to thy care, 'tis to my Mistress,
Conceal my lodgings, and do this for him
Will study noble Recompence.

DULCINO
You command me.

[Exit.

GRIMUNDO
What prettie youth is that? sure I have seen
That face before.

FOSCARI
Never; I brought him first
To Savoy, having rescu'd him from the
Bandetti, in my passage ore the Confines:
Is't not a sweet-fac'd thing? there are some Ladies
Might change their beauties with him.

GRIMUNDO
And gain by it.

FOSCARI
Nay, to his shape he has as fine a Soul,
Which graceth that perfection.

GRIMUNDO
You ha not
Been long acquainted with him?

FOSCARI
I have skill
In Phisnomy: believe my Character,
He's full of excellent sweetness.

GRIMUNDO
You express him
Passionately.

FOSCARI
His vertue will deserve

More praise, he suffers sit for love, in that
He is a Gentleman; for never could
Narrow and earthly minds be capable
Of Loves impression, or the injurie—
He willingly forsook his friends and Countrey,
Because unkindlie for unworthie ends,
They would have forc'd him marrie against his heart,
He told me so himself, and it were sin
Not to believe him: but omitting these,
How fares the best of Ladies, my Cleona?

GRIMUNDO
Your Cleona?

FOSCARI
Mine, she is in affection,
She is not married?

GRIMUNDO
No.

FOSCARI
She is in health?

GRIMUNDO
Yes.

FOSCARI
There is something in thy looks, I cannot
Read, be thy own gloss, and make me know
That doubtful Text, to whom hath she given up
The hope of my felicity, her heart,
Since my too fatal absence?

GIOTTO
Unto none,
Within the circle of my knowledge.

FOSCARI
Then
I am renew'd agen, may thy tongue never
Know sorrows accent.

GRIMUNDO
Will you presentlie.
Visit her?

FOSCARI

I have sent a letter, to
Certifie, I am still her loving servant.

GRIMUNDO
No matter, we'll be there before the boy,
There is necessity, if you knew all:
Come lets away.

FOSCARI
Agen thou dost afflict
My Soul with jealousie, if she have still
The clear possession of her heart.

GRIMUNDO
But you are
Dead Sir, remember that.

FOSCARI
I shall be living,
And soon enough present my self her fresh
And active Lover.

GRIMUNDO
If the Duke be not
Before you.

FOSCARI
How?

GRIMUNDO
The Duke, 'tis so resolv'd,
Your Rival, if you still affect Cleona,
Within this hour, he means his first sollicite
And personal siege; loose not your self with wonder,
If you neglect this opportunitie,
She having firm opinion of your death,
It will not be a miracle, if the Title
of Dutchess be a strong temptation
To a weak woman.

FOSCARI
I must thank your love,
And counsel, but for this time disingage
Your further stay with me, the Duke may miss you,
Preserve his favour, and forget me in
Your conference, I would be still conceal'd;
Let me consider on my fate, agen
I thank you, and dismiss you.

GRIMUNDO
Quiet thoughts
Dwell in your breast, in all things I obey you;
You know you have my heart.

[Exit.

FOSCARI
She's but a woman:
Yet how shall I be able to accuse her
With anie justice, when she thinks me dead.
The Duke, I must do something, I am full
Of discord, and my thoughts are fighting in me.
From our own Armie must arise one fear,
When Love it self is turn'd a Mutineer.

[Exit.

ACTUS II

SCENE I

The Same. A Room in Cleona's House.

Enter **JACOMO**, the **STEWARD**, and **SERVANTS**.

JACOMO
So, so, yet more perfume, y' are sweet Servingmen, make everie corner of the house smoke, bestir your selves, everie man know his Province, and be officious to please my Lady, according to his talent; have you furnisht out the banquet?

SERVANT
Most Methodicallie.

JACOMO
'Tis well, here should have been a fresh suit of Arras, but no matter, these bear the age well, let'em hang.

SERVANT
And there were a Mask to entertain his Highness?

JACOMO
Hang Masks, let everie conceit shew his own face, my Ladie would not disguise her entertainment, and now I talk of disguising, where's the Butler?

[Enter **BUTLER**.

BUTLER
Here Sir.

JACOMO
Where Sir? 'tis my Ladies pleasure that you be drunk to day, you will deal her Wine abroad the more liberallie among the Dukes servants, you are two tall Fellows, make good the credit of the Butterie, and when you are drunk, I will send others to relieve you: Go to your stations, if his Grace come hither a Sutor to my Ladie, as we have some cause to suspect, and after marrie her, I may be a great man, and ride upon a Reverend Moyle by patent, there is no end of my preferment; I did once teach my Ladie to dance, she must then teach me to rise: for indeed it is just, that only those, who get their living by their legs, should ride upon a Foot-cloth.

[Enter **SERVANT**.
SERVANT
Here's a young Gentleman desires to speak with my Ladie.

JACOMO
More young Gentlemen? tell him I am busie.

SERVANT
With my Ladie—

JACOMO
Busie with my Ladie Sir?

SERVANT
Would speak with my Ladie Sir?

JACOMO
I ha not done with my Ladie my self yet, he shall stay, 'tis for my Ladies State, no time to interrupt my Ladie; but now? I'le know his business, and taste it for my Ladie; if I like it, she shall hear more, but bid him come to me, methinks I talk like a peremptorie Statesman alreadie, I shall quicklie learn to forget my self when I am in great office; I will oppress the Subject, flatter the Prince, take bribes a both sides, do right to neitber, serve heaven as far as my profit will give me leave, and tremble onlie at the summons of a Parliament.

[Enter **DULCINO**.

Hum, a Page, a verie Page, one that would wriggle and prefer himself to be a Wag, 'tis so, have you anie letter of commendations?

DULCINO
I have a Letter Sir.

JACOMO
Let me see the complexion of the face, has it a handsom

Title Page, is it Stilo novo?

DULCINO
I have command Sir, to deliver it
To none but to my Ladie.

JACOMO
A forward Youth, I like him, he is not modest, I will assist his preferment, to engage him to my faction, a
special Courtpolicie, see my Ladie.

[Enter **CLEONA, ASTELLA, BELINDA**.

CLEONA
Yet stay Belinda—

BELINDA
I beseech you Madam
Allow excuse to my abrupt departure.
There is a business of much consequence,
And which you will not mourn to see effected.
Besides the dutie that I owe my Lord,
Compells me to it Madam.

CLEONA
Well, but that
We are acquainted with your vertue, this
Would move suspition you were not in
Charitie with the Duke.

BELINDA
You are pleasant Madam.

CLEONA
You are severe to bind yourself too strictlie
From Court and entertainments, sure your Lord
Should chide you for it.

ASTELLA [Aside to **BELINDA**]
If it please you stay,
Your Ladiship and I'le converse together,
My unkind Fate hath indisposed me,
To these State Ceremonies too.

BELINDA
You will oblige me by your pardon?

CLEONA
Use your pleasure.

ASTELLA
Nay you shall give me leave a little further,
Here I am useless.

[Exeunt **ASTELLA, BELINDA**.

JACOM0
May it please you Madam,
This prettie Gentleman has a suit to you,
And I in his behalf; he will be serviceable
And active in his place, a friend of mine.

DULCINO
Your Steward Madam is too full of zeal
To do me a preferment, but I have
No other ambition, than to commend
This paper to your white hands.

[Delivers the letter.

JACOM0
Never doubt,
'Tis done, be bold and call me fellow.

CLEONA
Be
You circumspect I pray, that all things have
Their perfect shape and order to receive
The Duke: you know our pleasure, not to spare
Or cost or studie to delight his highness.

JACOMO
I hope I have not been your Steward so long,
But I know how to put your Ladiship
To cost enough without studie.

[**CLEONA** reads.

CLEONA
Shall I credit
So great a bliss? the date is fresh, Foscari
Whom I thought dead? give him five hundred Crowns.

JACOMO [Aside to **DULCINO**]
We will divide em.

CLEONA

Stay.

JACOMO
You need not bid,
I use to make em stay, and long enough
Ere they receive such bounties.

CLEONA
Treasure is
Too cheap a payment for so rich a message.

JACOMO
This is the right Court largess.

CLEONA
The day breaks glorious to my darkned thoughts,
He lives, he lives yet; cease ye amorous fears,
More to perplex me: prethee speak sweet Youth,
How fares my Lord? upon my Virgin heart
I'le build a flaming Altar, to offer up
A thankful sacrifice for his Return
To life, and me; speak and increase my comforts:
Is he in perfect health?

DULCINO
Not perfect Madam, until you bless him with
The knowledge of your constancie.

CLEONA
O get thee wings and flie then,
Tell him my love doth burn like vestal fire,
Which with his memory, richer than all spices,
Dispersed odors round about my soul,
And did refresh it when 'twas dull and sad,
With thinking of his absence.

JACOMO
This is strange,
My Ladie is in love with him.

CLEONA
Yet stay,
Thou goest too soon away, where is he, speak?

DULCINO
He gave me no Commission for that Ladie,
He will soon save that question by his presence.

CLEONA
Time h'as no feathers, he walks now on crutches,
Relate his gesture when he gave thee this,
What other words, did mirth smile on his brow,
I would not for the wealth of this great world,
He should suspect my faith, what said he prethee?

DULCINO
He said, what a warm lover, whom desire
Makes eloquent could speak.

JACOMO
I have found it,
That boy comes from the Duke, that letter love,
'Twill be a match, and please your Ladiship—

CLEONA
Forbear your Ceremonies, what needs all this
Preparation, if the Duke vouchsafe
His person for my guest, dutie will teach me,
To entertain him without half this trouble;
I'le have no Ryot for his Highness.

JACOMO
Hum?
How's this?

CLEONA
Be less officious, you forget—
Sweet Youth, go forward with thy storie.

JACOMO
Hum?
This is a Fayrie, and the Devil sent him
To make my Ladie mad, 'twere well to trie
Whether he be flesh and blood, ha, I'le pinch him first.

[He pinches **DULCINO**, who starts.

CLEONA
How now?

JACOMO
My care shall see nothing be wanting, for
Your honour, and the Dukes.

CLEONA
Your place I see,

Is better than your manners, go too, be
Less troublesom, his Highness brings intents
Of grace, not burden to us, know your dutie.

JACOMO
So, I were best keep my self warm with my own office, while I may, the tyde is turn'd I see within two minutes, here was nothing but look to the Gallerie, perfume the Chambers, what Musick for the Duke, a Banquet for the Duke, now, be less officious, We'll have no Riot for his Highness, 'tis this Urchin h'as undone all our preferment.

CLEONA
The Suns lov'd flower, that shuts his yellow Curtain,
When he declineth, opens it again
At his fair rising, with my parting Lord,
I clos'd all my delights, till his approach,
It shall not spread it self.

[Enter **GENTLEMAN**.

GENTLEMAN
Madam the Duke?

CLEONA
Already.

[Enter **ASTELLA** and **LADIES**.

ASTELLA
He is entred.

CLEONA [To **DULCINO**]
Do not leave me,
I shall remember more.

[Enter **DUKE, FABRICHIO, SORANZO, GIOTTO**.

DUKE
Excellent Cleona.

CLEONA
The humble dutie of a Subject to your Highness.

[Kneels.

DUKE
Rise high in our thoughts, and thus
Confirm we are welcom, to these eyes, our heart,
Shall pay a lower dutie, than obedience

Hath taught your knee.

CLEONA
Your Grace much honours me,
Till this white hour, these walls were never proud,
T'inclose a guest, the genius of our house,
Is by so great a presence wak'd, and glories,
To entertain you.

DUKE
Everie accent falls
Like a fresh Jewel, to encrease her value,
We can but thank Cleona.

CLEONA
Royal Sir—

DUKE
Let me revoke that hastie syllable,
But thank thee; yes, we can do more, and will,
We have a heart to do't, our much griev'd Sister
I know you do not wear this sadness for
Our presence.

ASTELLA
If I've anie skill in mine own eys,
Since they beheld you, they have looked
More chearfullie, than they were wont.

DUKE
And yet I see a tear is readie to break prison.

ASTELLA
It is of joy to see you sir in health,
I hope the Prince is well?

DUKE
He will be so
Astella, when he leaves to be unkind
To thee, but let's forget him.

DULCINO
Fame ha's not
Injur'd him, in the character of his person.
And his shape promiseth a richer Soul,
I feel a new and fierie spirit dance,
Upon my heart-strings.

DUKE
We are come
My fair Cleona.

CLEONA
With your Highness pardon,
That name was never so attended, it
Becomes your bountie, but not me to wear
That Title.

DUKE
What?

CLEONA
Of fair my Lord?

DUKE
I said you were my fair Cleona—

CLEONA
Sir?

DUKE
I did apply,
I hope 't does not offend to call you so,
Y' are yet my Subject.

CLEONA
When I leave that name, may heaven—

DUKE
Be pleas'd to change it for a better.

CLEONA
It cannot.

DUKE
Do not sin, 'tis in our power
With your consent, to work that wonder Ladie.

CLEONA
I want my understanding.

DUKE
I'le explain,

CLEONA [Aside to **DULCINO**]
Do not believe him Youth, by all the faith

Of Virgins, I'le not change my service, to
Thy Master for his Dukedom.

DULCINO
Y' are too Noble.

DUKE
What boy is that? Ha! Giotto?

DULCINO
Madam, the Duke observes us.

DUKE
I ha seen him.
It is no common face.

SORANZO
My Lord we know not.

DUKE
Where is Grimundo?

GIOTTO
Not yet come my Lord.

DUKE
Send for him strait, and bid him bring the picture
We gave into his keeping, yet forbear,
It is in vain.

SORANZO
My Lord, Cleona waits
Your farther Courtship.

DUKE
Whither am I carried?

CLEONA
I hope, dread Sir, my house affords no object,
To interrupt your quiet.

DUKE
None but heavenly,
Or could this Roof be capable of ill,
Your onlie presence Ladie would convert it,
There is a vertuous magick in your eye.
For wheresoere it casts a beam, it does
Create a goodness, y'ave a handsom boy.

DULCINO [aside]
The Duke is troubled?

CLEONA
He's a prettie Youth.

DULCINO [aside]
I hope he wo'not take me from my Ladie,
I'le say I am her servant.

DUKE
Something binds
My speech, my heart is narrow of a sudden:
Giotto take some opportunitie
To enquire that Youths condition, name, and Countrey,
And give us private knowledge—[**SORANZO**
Whispers with **JACOMO**]—To cut off
Circumstance Ladie, I am not your fresh,
And unacquainted Lover, that doth waste

[**SORANZO** whispers with **JACOMO**.

The tedious Moons with preparation
To his amorous suit, I have been Cleona,
A long admirer of your Vertues, and
Do want the comfort of so sweet a partner,
In your young state.

CLEONA
You mock your humble hand-maid.

SORANZO
A stranger saist?

JACOMO
He brought some welcom letter
To my Ladie.

SORANZO
Not know his name, nor whence?

JACOMO
No my good Lord. So so, I like this well,
My Ladie does applie her to the Duke,
There is some hopes agen things may succeed;
This Lords discourcing with me, is an Omen
To my familiaritie to greatness.

DUKE

Grimundo not come yet? I am not well.

CLEONA

Good heaven defend, Angels protect your Highness.

DUKE

Your holie prayers cannot but do me good.
Continue that devotion, Charitie
Will teach you a consent to my departure.

CLEONA

I am unhappie.

DUKE

Make me not so Ladie
By the least trouble of your self; I am
Acquainted with these passions, let me breath
A heart upon thy lip—

[Kisses her.

Farewell, agen
Your pardon.

[Exit.

SORANZO

'Tis a verie strange distemper,
And sudden: Noble Ladie we must wait
Upon the Duke.

[Exeunt.

JACOMO

My bud is nipt agen,
Would all the banquet were in his bellie for't.

DULCINO

Let not my eyes betray me.

JACOMO

I'm sick too;
Let not your Ladiship repent your cost,
I'le have a care the sweet-meats be not lost.

[Exit.

CLEONA
Acquaint him with these passages of the Duke,
Tell him I long to see him, and at last,
To crown the storie, say my heart shall know
No other love but his.

DULCINO
I flie with this
Good news.

[Exit.

[Enter **JACOMO.**

JACOMO
Madam, here is Prince Lodwick.

CLEONA
Attend him.

JACOMO
Most officiously.

CLEONA
Stay, [whispers **ASTELLA**]—it can do no harm.

ASTELLA
E'en what you please.

CLEONA
If he enquire for his Lady, answer
She is not very well, and keeps her Chamber.

JACOMO
Ile say she's dead if you please, 'tis my duty:
Ile never speak truth while I live that shall
Offend your Ladiship.

[Exit.

CLEONA
You may hear all,
And when you please appear.

[**ASTELLA** retires.

[Enter **LODWICK** and **PIERO**.

LODWICK

Sick; where's her Doctor?
Ile be acquainted with him. Noble Lady.

CLEONA

Your Grace is here most welcome.

LODWICK

I am bold?

PIERO

I am happy that my duty to the Prince
Brought me to kisse your hand.

CLEONA

Beside the honour done to me, your person
Will add much comfort to Astella, your
Weak Lady.

LODWICK

She is sick; mend, let her mend, she'll spend her time worse, yet she knows my mind, and might do me the courtesie to die once; I'de take it more kindly, than to be at charge of a Physician.

CLEONA

You wo'd not poison her?

LODWICK

I think I must be driven to't; what shall a man do with a Woman that wo'not be ruled. I ha'given cause enough to break any reasonable womans heart in Savoy, and yet you see how I am troubled with her: but leave her to the Destinies. Where is my Brother all this while? I came to meet him; what, is't a match already? when shall we dance and triumph in the Tiltyard, for honour of the high and mightie Nuptials? where is he?

CLEONA

My Lord, he is gone.

LODWICK

How?

CLEONA

Distempered.

LODWICK

Not with Wine?

CLEONA

Departed sick.

LODWICK

She jeers him: By this lip Ile love thee, and thou wot abuse him; I knew he would but shame himself, and therefore durst not come with him for my own credit; I warrant he came fierce upon thee with some parcel of Poetry, which he had conn'd by heart out of Tasso, Guarrini, or some other of the same melting Tribe, and thought to have brought thy Maiden Town to his obedience, at the first noise of his furious Artillery.

CLEONA

My Lord, you understand me not, your Brother
Is not in health; some unkind pain within him
Compell'd him to forsake us.

LODWICK

Is it true
That he is sick? My Brother sick Piero.

PIERO

I am very well here.

1ST LADY

So am not I: pray sir appear more civil,
Or I shall leave you.

LODWICK

True?

CLEONA

'Tis too true my Lord.

LODWICK

No, no, Truth is a vertuous thing, and we cannot have too much on't. D'ye hear, if I may counsel you, be wise, and stay for me; you may be my Wife within this month, and the Dutchesse too.

CLEONA

Your Wife my Lord; why you are married,
What shall become of her?

LODWICK

Is she not sick?

CLEONA

But are you sure she'il die?

LODWICK

What a ridiculous question do you make: If death wo'not take a fair course with her, are there not reasons enough in State think you, to behead her; or if that seem cruel, because I do not affect blood, but for very good ends, I can be divorc'd from her, and leave her rich in the title of Lady Dowager.

CLEONA
Upon what offence can you pretend a divorce?

LODWICK
Because she is not fruitful; is not that a sin?

CLEONA
Would your Lordship have her fruitful, and you
Ne'r lie with her?

LODWICK
Have not I known a Lady, whose husband is an Eunuch upon Record, mother to three or four children, and no free conscience but commends her?

CLEONA
But these things wo'not be easily perfect, unlesse
You were Duke to enforce em.

LODWICK
Is not my Brother in the way? sick already, and perhaps as fit for heaven as another; I know he cannot live long, he's so well given, they never thrive, and then d'ye think Ile keep such a religious Court; in this corner lodge a Covy of Capouchins, who shall zealously pray for me without Stockins, in that a nest of Carthusians, things which in fine turn to Otters, appear flesh, but really are fish: No, no, give me a Court of flourishing pleasure, where delight in all her shapes, and studied varieties every minute courts the soul to act her chief felicity.

CLEONA
Do you never think of hell?

LODWICK
Faith I do, but it alwaies makes me melancholy, and therefore as seldome as I can my contemplation shall point thither; I am now in the spring of my life, winter will come on fast enough; when I am old, I will be as methodical an hypocrite, as any pair of Lawn Sleeves in Savoy.

CLEONA
I dare not hear him longer: Madam, release me.

[Enter **ASTELLA**.

LODWICK
How now; whence come you? were you sick?

ASTELLA
At heart my Lord, to think of your unkindnesse.

LODWICK

At heart: Ile ne'r believe without inspection. Am I unkind? go to, there's not a friend in the whole world can wish you better: Would you were canoniz'd a Saint, 'tis more than I wish my self yet; I do not trouble thee much on earth, and thou wert in heaven I would not pray to thee, for fear of disturbing thy Seraphical devotion.

ASTELLA
What sin have I committed deserves
This distance?

CLEONA
In Christian charitie salute her.

LODWICK
I would not have your Ladiship too ventrous,
The air is somewhat cold, and may endanger
A weak body.

ASTELLA
If the suspicion that I am unchaste—

LODWICK
Unchaste; By this hand I do not know an honest woman in the Dukedome.

CLEONA
How, my Lord: what do ye think of me?

LODWICK
I know not whether you be a woman or no, yet.

CLEONA
Fie, my Lord.

LODWICK
What would you have me do? I have not seen her this six months.

ASTELLA
O rather, my Lord, conclude my sufferings,
Than thus with tortures lengthen out my death:
Oh kill me, and I beseech you; I will kisse
The instrument, which guided by your hand,
Shall give my grief a period, and pronounce

[Enter **GRIMUNDO**.

With my last breath your free forgivenesse.

LODWICK
No, kill your self, more good will come on't: how now? nay then w'are like to have a precious time on't.

CLEONA

The Duke, my Lord, enquired for you.

GRIMUNDO

I met
His Highnesse in return, and he imploy'd me
To bring back knowledge of his better health;
Which, he says, shall enable him but to
Expresse how much he honours fair Cleona.

CLEONA

I am his studious servant, and rejoice
In this good news: Your Brother is recovered.

LODWICK

I, I, I knew he would do well enough: Now sir?

GRIMUNDO

I have some businesse with you, my Lord,
Were you at opportunity.

LODWICK

Some moral exhortations; they are fruitlesse: I shall never eat Garlick with Diogenes in a Tub, and speculate the Stars without a Shirt: Prithee enjoy thy Religion, and live at last most Philosophical lousie.

GRIMUNDO

My design is of another nature.

CLEONA

May I obtain so great a favour Sir,
You'd be my guest in absence of the Duke;
I'm but ambitious to remember
His health in Greek Wine.

LODWICK

So this Lady will be temperate, and use me but like a Stranger, without pressing me to inconveniences of kissing her, and other superstitious Courtship of a husband.

CLEONA

I will engage she'll not offend you.

LODWICK

And yet it goes against my conscience to tarrie so long in honest companie; but my comfort is, I do not use it. Come away Piero, you have had a fine time on't.

CLEONA

My Lord.

GRIMUNDO
I follow Madam, yet have comfort,
Though reason and example urge our fears,
Heaven will not let you lose so many tears.

[Exeunt.

Foscari's Lodgings.

[Enter **FOSCARI**, and **DULCINO**.

FOSCARI
Did she receive my Letter with such joy?

DULCINO
I want expression, my Lord, to give you
The circumstance; with what a flowing love,
Or rather, with what glad devotion
She entertain'd it; at your very name,
For so I ghest, to which her covetous sight
Made the first haste; one might have seen her heart
Dance in her eies, and as the wonder strove
To make her pale, warm love did fortifie
Her cheeks with guilty blushes, she did read
And kisse the paper often.

FOSCARI
This was before the Duke came thither?

DULCINO
Yes, my Lord.

FOSCARI
And didst thou not
Observe her at his presence lack that fervour
Her former passion had begot of me?
Was she not courtlie to him, Boy?

DULCINO
So far
As her great birth and breeding might direct
A Lady to behave her self to him, that was her Prince.

FOSCARI
She kiss'd him, did she not?

DULCINO
She kiss'd.

FOSCARI
He did salute her?

DULCINO
Yes, my Lord.

FOSCARI
And didst not see a flame hang on her lip,
A spirit busie to betray her love,
And in a sigh conveigh it to him? Oh
Thou canst not read a woman. Did he not
Wooe her to be his Dutchesse?

DULCINO
Yes, my Lord.

FOSCARI
Thou shouldst ha watcht her cheek then; there a blush
Had been a guilt indeed, a feeble answer,
With half a smile, had been an argument
She had been lost, and the temptation
Above her strength; which had I known, I could
Have slept, and never been disturb'd, although
I had met her in a dream.

DULCINO
My Lord, you weave a causeless trouble to your self.

FOSCARI
Oh jealousie. I am asham'd—

DULCINO
If ever any woman lov'd
With faith, Cleona honours you above
Mankind; 'twere sin, but to suspect so chaste,
So furnish'd with all vertue, your Cleona.

FOSCARI
It were indeed; I am too blame Dulcino;
Yet when thou comst to be so ripe, for so
Much miserie, as to love, thou wo't excuse me.

DULCINO

My Lord, if I might not offend with my
Opinion, it were safest that you lose
No time, your presence would confirm a joy
To either, and prevent the Duke, whose strong
Solicits may in time endanger much
The quiet of your thoughts.

FOSCARI

O never, never, and I will reward
Her love beyond example: Thus Dulcino
Thou shalt return.

DULCINO

My Lord, I had much rather
Write on you to her.

FOSCARI

Tush, thou understandst not
What I have purpos'd, thou shalt presentlie
Go back, and tell Cleona I am dead.

DULCINO

How, dead?

FOSCARI

I boy, that I am dead: nay, mark the issue.

DULCINO

But my Lord, she hath your Letter
To check that.

FOSCARI

Thou shalt frame something to take
That off, some fine invention may be made,
To say 'twas forg'd, we'll studie that anon,
In the assurance of my death, which must
Be so delivered, as she shall believe thee,
She may affect the Duke.

DULCINO

Ho sir, the Duke?

FOSCARI

I, I, the Duke: for that's the plot, I must advance.

DULCINO

And will you thus reward so great a love to you?

FOSCARI

Best, best of all,
Shall I be so ungrateful to a Ladie
Of such rare merit, when a Prince desires
To make her great? by my unworthie interest
Destroy her blessings, hinder such a fortune
From fair Cleona? Let her love the Duke;
In this I will expresse the height and glorie
Of my best service.

DULCINO

Are you sir in earnest?

FOSCARI

I love her, and can never see her more:
Posteritie shall learn new pietie
In love from me; it will become me look on
Cleona a far off, and only mention
Her name, as I do Angels in my prayer:
Thus she deserves I should converse with her;
Thus I most nobly love her.

DULCINO

Doth she languish
Expecting you, and shall I carrie death
To comfort her? good heaven forbid this Sir.

FOSCARI

Heaven doth engage me to it: she shall
Reign glorious in power, while I let fall my Beads
That she might prosper. Be not thou an enemy
To her and me, but do it, or never see more.

[Exit.

DULCINO

I'm lost i'th springing of my hope, shall I
Obey him, to destroy my self? I must,
I dare not be my self; no need have they
Of other force, that make themselves away?

[Exit.

ACTUS III

A Room in Cleona's House.

Enter **JACOMO**.

JACOMO
I smell a Match agen: the Duke will fetch her about; here was another Ambassadour at dinner, and his Highnesse is again expected: in confidence of my place that shall be, I will continue my state posture, use my Tooth-pick with discretion, and cough distinctly: what can hinder my rising? I am no Schollar, that exception is taken away; for most our States-men do hold it a saucy thing, for any of their Servants to be wiser than themselves.

[Enter **DULCINO**.

DULCINO
Worthy Sir—

JACOMO
My Lady shall be at leisure for you presently—
It may be you would speak with me first?

DULCINO
I only entreat my Lady may have knowledge
That I wait here.

JACOMO
I will enrich my Ladies understanding; Ile say nothing else, but that you are here, shall I? That's enough if you have another Letter.

DULCINO
What then?

JACOMO
I would wish you deliver it to her own hand: but under your favour, the Contents of the last Chapter had like to undone us all, and Cupid had not bin more merciful.

DULCINO
Fear nothing, the news I bring will make you merrie.

JACOMO
I'de laugh at that; howsoever you are heartilie welcome, and ever shall be: You do hear no harm of the Duke?

DULCINO
No harm?

JACOMO

You shall hear more shortly: I say no more, but heaven bless my Ladie and his Highnesse together, for my part, though I speak a proud word—I'le tell my Ladie that you attend her.

DULCINO
I prithee do, and hasten the discharge
Of my sad Embassie, which when I have done,
And that it prospers in mine own misfortune,
I'le teach my breath to pray.

[Enter **CLEONA, FABRICHIO, JACOMO**.

FABRICHIO
A glorious fate
Courts your acceptance, and I hope your wisdom
Will teach you how to meet it, y'ave receiv'd
His Highness bosom, now Ile take my leave.

CLEONA
Will you not see the Prince again?

FABRICHIO
I saw his highnesse walking with Grimundo
Toward the garden, and the Duke expects me—
Think of a Dutches Madam.

CLEONA
I'me not worthy,
And needs must sink under the weight of such
A title; my humblest service to his grace,
I am his beads-woman.

[Exit **FABRICHIO**.

JACOMO
Madam here's the youth.

CLEONA
Art thou return'd already? why were you
So rude to make him waite?

DULCINO
Since I arriv'd
'Tis but a pair of minutes.

CLEONA
They are worth
As many dayes.

JACOMO
He shall be with your Ladiship
Next time before he come; when I but spye him
A mile off, Ile acquaint you in my duty
To your self, and my honour unto him.

CLEONA
Withdraw.

JACOMO
Here is no couth, I do not like
My Ladies familiarity with a boy:
Methinks a man were fitter, and more able
To give her a refreshing: but this Lobby
Shall be my next remove.

[Exit, and stays behind the hangings.

DULCINO
You will repent
This welcom Madam.

CLEONA
What harsh sound is that?
Thy looks upon a suddain are become
Dismal, thy brow dull as Saturns issue;
Thy lips are hung with black, as if thy tongue
Were to pronounce some funeral.

DULCINO
It is,
But let your vertue place a guard about
Your eare; it is too weak a sence to trust
With a sad tale, that may disperse too soon
The killing sillables, and some one or other
Find out your heart.

CLEONA
The Mandrake hath no voice
Like this, the Raven and the night birds sing
More soft, nothing in nature, to which fear
Hath made us superstitious, but speak gently
Compar'd with thee; discharge thy fatall burthen,
I am prepar'd, or stay but answer me,
I will and save thy breath, and quickly know
The total of my sorrow; is Foscari
Dead since I saw thee last? or hath some wound,
Or other dire mis-fortune seal'd him for

The grave? that though he yet live, I may bid
My heart despair to see him.

DULCINO
None of these,
Since last I saw you Madam.

CLEONA
None of these?
Then I despise all sorrow boy, there is
Not left another mischief in my Fate;
Call home thy beauty, why dost look so pale?
See I am arm'd, and can with valiant blood
Hear thee discourse of my terror now;
Methinks I can in the assurance of
His safety, hear of Battails, Tempest, death,
With all the horrid shapes that Poets fancy;
Tell me the tale of Troy or Rome on fire,
Rich in the trophies of the conquered world,
I will not shed so many tears to save
The Temples, as my joy doth sacrifice
To hear my Lord is well.

DULCINO
Turn them to grief
Agen, and here let me kneele, the accuser
Of him, that hath deserv'd more punishment,
Than your wrong'd piety will inflict.

CLEONA
Dost kneele, and call thy self accuser?

DULCINO
Yes.

CLEONA
Of whom,
Thy Lord? take heed, for if I be thy judge
I shall condemn thee ere thou speak.

DULCINO
You may,
But I accuse my self, and of an injury
To you.

CLEONA
To me?

DULCINO
Too great to be forgiven.

CLEONA
My love to him thou serv'st hath found a pardon
Already for it; be it an offence
Against my life.

DULCINO
For his sake you must punish,
Dear Madam, I have sinn'd against his ghost,
In my deceiving you.

CLEONA
His Ghost?

DULCINO
And if
His soul had not forgotten how he loved you,
I must expect him to afright my dreams,
The truth is, my Lord is dead.

CLEONA
How dead? when? where? did I
Not hear thee say, since I receiv'd this letter,
He was alive?

DULCINO
No Madam.

CLEONA
Be not impious.

DULCINO
I said that neither death, nor any black
Misfortune had befalne him, since I gave
The letter to you.

CLEONA
Grant this truth, I am secur'd agen.

DULCINO
'Las he was dead before,
I'm sure you could not choose but hear as much,
It was my wickedness arriv'd to mock
Your credulous heart with a devised letter:
I know you are in wonder what should move me
To this imposture; sure it was no malice,

For you nere injur'd me, and that doth make
My crime the more deform'd, all my aime was,
Being a stranger here, and wanting means
After my Lords death, by this cunning to
Procure some bounty from you to sustain
My life, until by some good fortune, I
Might get another Master, for I knew
There was no hope to benefit my self
By saying he was dead: good heaven forgive me,
And keep my eys from weeping,

CLEONA
Thou hast undone me,
Like a most cruel boy.

DULCINO
Madam I hope
I shall repair the ruines of your eye,
When I declare the cause that leades me to
This strange confession; I have observ'd
The Duke does love you, love you in that way,
You can deserve him, and though I have sinn'd,
I am not stubborn in my fault to suffer you
In the belief of my deceitful story,
To wrong your fortune by neglect of him
Can bring your merit such addition
Of state and title.

CLEONA
Dost thou mock agen?

DULCINO
Heaven knows I have no thought of such impiety,
If you will not believe that for your sake
I have betrayed my self, yet be so charitable,
To think it something of my duty to
The Duke, whose ends, while they are just and noble,
All loyal subjects ought to serve for him,
Whom I am not bound to honour, and I love him,
Else may I never know one day of comfort;
I durst not without guilt of treason to
His chaste desires deceive you any longer:
Collect your self dear Madam, in the grave
There dwells no musick, in the Dukes embrace
You meet a perfect happinesse.

CLEONA
Begon,

And never see me more; who ever knew
Falsehood so ripe at thy years?

[Exit.

DULCINO
Is not yet
My poor heart broke? hath nature given it
So strong a temper that no wound will kill me?
What charm was in my gratitude to make me
Undoe so many comforts with one breath?
Or was it for some sin I had to satisfie?
I have not only widowed Cleona,
But made my self a misery beneath
An Orphant; I nere came to have a friend,
I ha destroy'd my hope, that little hope
I had to be so happy.

[JACOMO comes forth.

JACOMO
Is't e'ne so?

My friend what make you here? who sent for you? begon dee hear, begon I say the word too; there is a
Porters lodge else, where you may have due chastisement, youle begon.

DULCINO
I'm sorry
I have offended Sir,

[Exit **DULCINO**

JACOMO
So am not I;

Let me see some body is dead, if I knew who, no matter 'tis one that my Lady lov'd, and I am glad to
hear it for mine own sake; now Venus speed the Dukes plough, and turn me loose to a privy Councellor.

[Enter **SORANZO**.

SORANZO
Signior Jacomo, where's your Lady?

JACOMO
She is within my good Lord, wilt please you walk this way?

SORANZO
Prethee make haste, the Duke is coming.

[Exeunt.

Another Room in the Same.

JACOMO
I smell him hitherto.

[Enter **JACOMO** presently.

So so, I will take this opportunitie to present my self to his Highness, that he may take particular notice of my bulk and personage, he may chance speak to me, I have common places to answer any ordinarie question, and for other, he shall find by my impudence, I come not short of a perfect Courtier. Here he comes, I will dissemble some contemplation, and with my Hat on, give him cause to observe me the better.

[Enter the **DUKE**, **GRIMUNDO**, **GIOTTO** and **LORDS**.

DUKE
What fellow's that?

GIOTTO
A servant of Cleona's.

[The **DUKE** extends his hand, **JACOMO** kisses it.

FABRICHIO
Signior?

JACOMO
Your Highness humble creature, you have blest my lips, and I will wear them thred-bare with my prayers for your Graces immortal prosperitie.

[Enter **SORANZO**.

DUKE
Soranzo is return'd: How fares Cleona?

SORANZO
My Lord, not well, I found her full of sadness, which is encreast, she cannot, as becomes her dutie, observe your Highness.

JACOMO
One word with your Grace in private; she is as well, as either you or I.

DUKE
Saist thou so?

JACOMO
There came indeed certain news before you, that a noble Gentleman, I know not who, and therefore he shall be nameless, but some dear friend of hers is dead, and that's all, and that hath put her into a melanchollie mood; with your gracious pardon, if I were worthie to be one of your Counsellors.—

DUKE
What then?

JACOMO
I would advise you, as others do, to take your own course; your Grace knows best what is to be done.

DUKE
So sir: Didst thou not see the prettie boy I told thee of?

SORANZO
No my good Lord.

DUKE
We are resolv'd to comfort her; set forward.

GRIMUNDO
You had simple grace.

JACOMO
A touch or so, a beam with which his Highness
Doth use to keep desert warm: good my Lord,
It is not come to that yet.

[Exeunt **GRIMUNDO** followed by **JACOMO**.

SCENE III

Foscari's Lodgings.

[Enter **FOSCARI** and a **SERVANT**.

FOSCARI
Go to the next religious house, and pray
Some holy father come and speak with me:
But hasten thy Return.

[Exit **SERVANT**.

I must not entertain with the same thought
Cleona, and my love, lest my own passion
Betray the Resolution I ha made
To make my service famous to all ages.
A legend that may startle wanton blood,
And strike a chilness in the active veins
Of noblest lovers, when they hear, or read,
That to advance a Mistress, I have given her
From mine own heart, if anie shall be so
Impious at my memorie, to say
I could not do this act, and love her too,
Some power divine, that knew how much I lov'd her,
Some Angel that hath care to right the dead,
Punish that crime for me, he is come.

[Enter **VALENTIO**, a religious man.

Welcom good father;
I sent to intreat your help, but first, pray tell me,
I have no perfect memorie, what Saint
Gives title to your Order?

VALENTIO
We do wear
The Scapular of St. Bennet Sir.

FOSCARI
Your Charitie
Make you still worthie of that Reverend habit,
I have a great devotion, to be made
A brother of your sacrèd institution:
What persons of great birth it hath receiv'd?

VALENTIO
To fashion my Reply to your demand,
Is not to boast, though I proclaim the honours
Of our profession; four Emperors,
Fortie six Kings, and one and fiftie Queens,
Have chang'd their Royal Ermines for our sables,
These Cowls have cloth'd the heads of fourteen hundred,
And six Kings sons, of Dukes, great Marquises,
And Earls, two thousand and above four hundred
Have turn'd their Princelie Coronets, into
An humble Coronet of hair left by
The Razor thus.

[Pointing to his tonsure.

FOSCARI
This, it is not.
There is a Sun ten times more glorious,
Than that which riseth in the East, attracts me
To feed upon his sweet beams, and become
A Bird of Paradise, a Religious man
To rise from earth, and no more to turn back,
But for a Burial.

VALENTIO
Think what 'tis you do,
It is nothing to play the wanton with,
In the strong bended passion of an humor,
For a friends death, a Kings frown, or perhaps
Loss of a Mistress.

FOSCARI
O still bless the guide
Whatever, that shall lead this happie way.

VALENTIO
My Lord, the truth is like your Coat of Arms,
Richest when plainest; I do fear the world
Hath tyr'd you, and you seek a Cell to rest in,
As Birds that wing it o're the Sea, seek ships,
Till they get breath, and then they flie away.

FOSCARI
Do not mistake a pietie, I am prepar'd,
And can endure your strict mortifications.
Good Father then prefer my humble suit,
To your Superior for the habit, and
Let me not long expect you, say I am,
Noble, but humblest in my thoughts.

VALENTIO
I go,
Mean time examine well this new desire,
Whether it be a wild flash, or a heavenlie fire.

[Exit.

[Enter **DULCINO**.

FOSCARI
Now my good Boy.

DULCINO

Sir, your command is done,
And she believes?

FOSCARI

That I am dead Dulcino?

DULCINO

That you are dead, and as she now scorn'd life
Death lends her cheeks his paleness, and her eyes
Tell down their drops of silver to the earth,
Wishing her tears might Rain upon your Grave,
To make the gentle earth produce some flower,
Should bear your names and memories.

FOSCARI

But thou seest,
I live Dulcino.

DULCINO

Sir, I should be blest,
If I did see you sought the means to live,
And to live happilie, O noble sir
Let me untread my steps, unsay my words,
And tell your love, you live.

FOSCARI

No my sweet boy,
She thinks not much amiss, I am a man
But of an hour or two; my will is made
And now I go, never more chearfullie,
To give eternal farewell to my friends.

DULCINO

For heavens sake sir, what's this you mean to do?
There is a fear sits cold upon my heart,
And tells me—

FOSCARI

Let it not misinform thee boy;
I'le use no violence to my self, I am
Resolv'd a course, wherein I will not doubt,
But thou wilt bear me companie? we'll enter
Into Religion.

DULCINO

Into Religion?

FOSCARI
O'tis a heavenlie life, go with me Boy,
We'll imitate the singing Angels there,
Learn how to keep a Quire in heaven, and scorn
Earths transitorie glorie; wo't Dulcino?

DULCINO
Alas my Lord, I am too young.

FOSCARI
Too young
To serve heaven? Never, never; O take heed
Of such excuse.

DULCINO
Alas, what shall I do?
And yet I'me wearie of the world, but how
Can I do this? I am not yet discovered: [aside]
Sir, I shall still attend you.

FOSCARI
Thou art my comfort,
I have propounded it alreadie, to
A Benedictine, by whose means we may
Obtain the habit; stay thou and expect him,
I must be absent for a little time,
To finish something, will conduce to my
Eternal quiet, if th'hast anie scruple,
He will direct thee, having both made even
With earth, we'll travail hand in hand to heaven.

[Exit.

DULCINO
Fortune hath lent me a prospective glass,
By which I have a look beyond all joyes,
To a new world of miserie, what's my best
Let it be so, for I am hopeless now,
And it were well, if when those weeds I have,
That I might go disguised to my grave.

[Exit.

SCENE IV

A Room in Cleona's House.

[Enter **LODWICK** and **GRIMUNDO**.

LODWICK
This is strange.

GRIMUNDO
You know I have given you manie precepts of honestie?

LODWICK
And you know how I have followed em.

GRIMUNDO
To mine own heart, I have made tedious discourses of heaven to ye, and the Moral Vertues, numbred up the duties of a good Prince, urg'd examples of vertues for your imitation.

LODWICK
To much purpose.

GRIMUNDO
Seem'd to sweat with agonie and vexation, for your obstinate courses reprov'd you, nay, sometimes made complaints of you to the Duke.

LODWICK
And I ha'curst you for it, I remember.

GRIMUNDO
Alas my Lord, I durst do no otherwise: was not the Duke your father an honest man? and your brother now foolishlie takes after him, whose credulities, when I had alreadie cozened, I was bound to appear Stoical, to preserve the opinion they had conceived of me.

LODWICK
Possible.

GRIMUNDO
It speaks discretion and abilities in States-men, to apply themselves to their Princes disposition, varie a thousand shapes; if he be honest, we put on a formal of gravitie; if he be vitious, we are Parasites. Indeed in a politique Commonwealth, all things are but Representation, and my Lord, howsoever I have appear'd to you, I am at heart one of your own Sect, an Epicure; be but so subtle to seem honest, as I do, and we will laugh at the foolish world in our Cells, déclaim against intemperate livers, and hug our own licentiousness, while we surfet our souls in the dark with Nectar and Ambrosia.

LODWICK
Can this be earnest, you did talk of hell, and bug-bears?

GRIMUNDO
I confess, and were you in publick, I would urge manie other emptie names to fright you, put on my holie-day countenance, and talk nothing but Divinitie, and golden sentences.

LODWICK

You were a Christian, how came you to be converted?

GRIMUNDO

I think I had a name given me, and that's all I retain; I could never endure reallie their severe discipline: Marrie for my preferment, and other politique ends, I have, and can still dispense with fasting, prayer, and a thousand fond austerities, though I do penance for em in private.

LODWICK

Let me ask you one question, were you never drunk?

GRIMUNDO

A thousand times in my studie, that's one of my Recreations.

LODWICK

How chance I could never see't in you? you know I would ha'been drunk for companie.

GRIMUNDO

But I durst not trust so young a sinner; for I always held it a maxim, to do wickedness with circumspection.

LODWICK

Wickedness?

GRIMUNDO

I speak in the phrase of the foolish world, that holds voluptuousness a crime, which you and I, and everie'wise man knows to be the onlie happiness of life, and the inheritance we are born to.

LODWICK

But stay, how comes it to pass, that accounting me so young a sinner, you now adventure to discover your self?

GRIMUNDO

To you?

LODWICK

To me.

GRIMUNDO

Good my Lord conceive me, you were a young sinner, and in your Nonage, does that infer that you have made no growth, that y'are a Child still, dee think that I ha not wit to distinguish a Principiant in vice, from a Graduate, shall I be afraid to lay open my secret impieties to you, that are almost as perfect as my self in Epicurism?

LODWICK

Verie well, proceed.

GRIMUNDO

And yet my Lord, with your Princelie licence, you may learn too, and indeed the first vertue that I would commend to your practice, should be that, by which I have attain'd to this height, and opinion, and that's hypocrisie.

LODWICK

Hypocrisie?

GRIMUNDO

Yes, a delicate white Devil, do but fashion your self to seem holie, and studie to be worse in private, worse, you'll find your self more active in your sensualitie, and it will be another titillation, to think what an Ass you make a'the believing world, that will be readie to dote, nay, superstitiouslie adore you, for abusing them.

LODWICK

This is prettie wholsom doctrine, and hark you, ha you no wenches now and then?

GRIMUNDO

Wenches? would the Duke your brother had so manie for his own sake, or you either.

LODWICK

Hast i'faith?

GRIMUNDO

Why judge by your self, how dee think a Gentleman should subsist? I'le not give a Chip to be an Emperour, and I may not curvet as often as my constitution requires. Wenches, why I have as manie— yet now I think better on't, I'le keep that to my self, store makes a good proverb.

LODWICK

Nay, nay, be free and open to me, you have my oath not to betray.

GRIMUNDO

Well, I'le not be nice to you, you little imagine (though I be married that I am the greatest Whoremaster i'th' Dukedom.

LODWICK

Not the greatest?

GRIMUNDO

Have a strong faith, and save my proofs; but Caute si non Caste, my Nun at home knows nothing, like a Mole in the earth, I work deep, but invisible; I have my private houses, my Granaries, my Magasines Bullie, as manie Concubines, as would, collected, furnish the Great Turks Seraglio.

LODWICK

How do you conceal em? I should nere keep half so manie, but 'twould be known.

GRIMUNDO

You are then a Novice in the Art of Uenus, and will tell Tales out a' the School, like your weak gallants o' the first Chin, that will bragge what Ladies they have brought to their obedience, that think it a mightie honour, to discourse how many Forts they have beleaguer'd; how many they have taken by batterie; how many by composition, and how many by stratagem: a fine commendation for young whelps, is't not?

LODWICK
A fault, a fault; who can deny it? But what are those you practice with? A touch, come.

GRIMUNDO
Not sale-ware, Mercenary stuff; but rich, fair, highfed, glorious, Ladies of blood; whose eys will make a souldier melt, and he were compos'd of marble; whose very smile hath a magnetick force to draw souls; whose voice will charm a Satyr, and turn a mans prayer into ambition.

LODWICK
I have heard you; and now I think fit to discover my self to you: You are a Rascal.

GRIMUNDO
Sir, I think I am one.

LODWICK
Let not your Wisdome think, I can be so easilie gull'd.

GRIMUNDO
How Sir?

LODWICK
You think you have talked very methodicallie, and cunninglie all this while, and that I am, as they say, a credulous Coxcomb, and cannot perceive, that by your politique jeers upon my pleasures, you labour to discredit, not onlie my recreations, but my self to my own face: D'ye hear? the time may come you will not dare these things, and yet you shall see, I will not now so much as seem angrie: preserve your humour, 'twill appear fresh o'th'Stage, my learned Gymnosophist; verie well, excellent well.

GRIMUNDO
Why does not your Lordship believe me then?

LODWICK
Do'st thou think throughout the year, I will lose one minute of my pastime, for this your toothlesse Satyr? I'le to a Wench presentlie.

GRIMUNDO
I came to carrie you to one.

LODWICK
How, thou?

GRIMUNDO
Do not deceive your self; come, you shall believe, and thank me: go with me, and I will demonstrate.

LODWICK
Whither?

GRIMUNDO
I'le carrie you to a Ladie; be not afraid, she is honest; such a charming brow, speaking eie, springing cheek, tempting lip, swelling bosome.

LODWICK
Will you lead me to such a creature?

GRIMUNDO
Yes.

LODWICK
And shall I?

GRIMUNDO
And think your self richer, than to be Lord of both the Indies; here's my hand, cut it off, if I do not this feat for you when you please; and when you are satisfied with her, I'le help you to fortie more: but we are interrupted.

[Enter **GIOTTO, SORANZO**.

GIOTTO
There he is with Grimundo.

SORANZO
His late Governour, he is giving him good counsell.

GIOTTO
Pray heaven he have the grace to follow it.

GRIMUNDO
Consider Sir, what will be the end
Of all these wicked courses.

LODWICK [aside]
Precious Villain.

GRIMUNDO
We must be circumspect.

LODWICK
No more: I have a crotchet new sprung:
Where shall I meet thee?

GRIMUNDO

I'le expect you in the Park—be very secret.
My Lord, I can but grieve for you.

[Exit.

LODWICK
How have we all been couzen'd? [Aside]
What, is my Brother here?

SORANZO
This hour, my Lord, he is now upon return.

LODWICK
I'le see him, and then prepare me for this Ladie.
I feel a boiling in my veins alreadie;
This is the life of greatnesse, and of Court;
They're fools that will be frighted from their sport.

[Exeunt.

SCENE I

A Room in Cleona's House.

Enter **LODWICK** and **PIERO**.

LODWICK
Do't and thou lov'st me.

PIERO
What d'ye mean, my Lord?

LODWICK
Nay, we must have such a deal of circumstance; I say, do it.

PIERO
What, that?

LODWICK
That: is that such a piece of matter, does it appear so horrid in your imagination, that you should look as if you were frighted now?

PIERO
My Lord, it is—

LODWICK

A thing your heat will prompt you to, but that you affect ceremonie, and love to be entreated.

PIERO

With your Ladie?

LODWICK

Yet again: you have not been observ'd so dull in a businesse of this supple nature.

PIERO

But think on'c agen; I pray you think a little better: I ha no great ambition to ha my throat cut.

LODWICK

By whom?

PIERO

By you; you cannot chuse but kill me for't when I have done. Your Ladie?

LODWICK

Is your mountanous promise come to this? Remember; if I do not turn honest—

PIERO

My Lord, do but consider—well, I will do what I can, and there be no remedie—but

LODWICK

Never fear it, for if thou canst but corrupt her, I'le sue a Divorce presentlie.

PIERO

And bring me in for a witness?

[Enter **ASTELLA**.

LODWICK

She's here; fear nothing, I'le be thy protection; it were not amisse to cast away some kindness upon her: nay, I was coming to take my leave.

ASTELLA

I know you never meant it.

LODWICK

Thus my best intents are rewarded still, the more sin upon your conscience; y'have a hard heart, but heaven forgive us all: Astella farewell; Piero expect my return here—pray entertain this Gentleman courteouslie in my absence, you know not how kindlie I may take it.

ASTELLA

I would you would enjoyn me any testimonie,
So I may be in hope to win your love.

LODWICK
'Tis in the will of women to do much; do not despair; the proudest heart is but flesh, think a that.

ASTELLA
Of what?

LODWICK
Of flesh; and so I leave you.

[Exit.

PIERO
Will't please you Madam walk into your Chamber?
I have something to impart will require more privacie.

ASTELLA
If it be grief 'tis welcome.

[Exeunt.

SCENE II

A Room in the Duke's Palace

[Enter **DUKE** and **LORDS**.

DUKE
My soul I have examin'd, and yet find
No reason for my foolish passion.
Out hot Italian doth affect these boys
For sin; I've no such flame, and yet methought
He did appear most lovely; nay, in his absence,
I cherish his idea; but I must
Exclude him while he hath but soft impression;
Being removed already in his person,
I lose him with less trouble [aside]

[Enter **GIOTTO**.

GIOTTO
Please your Highness,
A Stranger, but some Gentleman of qualitie,
Intending to leave Savoy, humbly prays
To kisse your hand.

DUKE
A Gentleman: admit him.

[Enter **FOSCARI** disguised, and kisses the **DUKE'S** hand.

FOSCARI
You are a gracious Prince, and this high favour
Deserves my Person and my Sword, when you
Vouchsafe so much addition to this honour,
To call them to your service.

DUKE
You are Noble.

FOSCARI
It is not complement my Lord alone,
Made me thus bold; I have a private message,
Please you command their distance.

DUKE
Wait without.

[Exeunt **LORDS**.

FOSCARI
Have you forgot this face?

[Discovers himself.

DUKE
Foscari's shadow.

FOSCARI
The substance, Sir, and once more at your feet.

DUKE
Return'd to life. Rise; meet cut arms: why in
This Cloud?

FOSCARI
Your pardon, Royal Sir; it will
Concern your Hignesse to permit me walk
In some Eclipse.

DUKE
How?

FOSCARI

I said I had a message:
I come from Cleona.

DUKE
From Cleona?

FOSCARI
And in her name I must
Propound a question; to which she prays
You would be just and noble in your answer.

DUKE
Without disputing your Commission,
Upon mine honour—

FOSCARI
Princes cannot stain it: D'ye love her;

DUKE
Do I love her? Strange.

FOSCARI
Nay, she would have you pause, and think well e'r
You give her resolution; for she bid me tell you,
She has been much afflicted since you left her, about your love.

DUKE
About my love? I prithee be more particular.

FOSCARI
I shall: So soon as you were gone, being alone, and full
Of melancholie thoughts.

DUKE
I left her so.

FOSCARI
Willing to ease her head upon her Couch,
Through silence, and some friendship of the dark,
She fell asleep, and in a short dream thought
Some Spirit told her softly in her ear,
You did but mock her with a smoo h pretence
Of love.

DUKE
Ha!

FOSCARI

More; that you were fallen from honour,
Have taken impious flames into your bosome;
That y'are a bird of prey, and while she hath
No houshold Lar, to wait upon her threshold,
You would flie in, and seize upon her honour.

DUKE
I hope she hath no faith in dreams.

FOSCARI
She cannot tell; she hath some fears, my Lord;
Great men have left examples of their vice:
If you but once more say you love Cleona,
And speak it unto me, and to the Angels,
Which in her prayers she hath invok'd to hear you,
She will be confident.

DUKE
Though I need not
Give an account to any, but to heaven
And her fair self. Foscari thou shalt tell her
With what alacritie I display my heart:
I love her with chaste and noble fire; my intents are
Fair as her brow: tell her I dare proclaim it
In my devotions, at that minute when
I know a millon of adoring Spirits
Hover about the Altar: I do love her—

FOSCARI
Enough: my Lord, be pleas'd to hear
What I have now to say; You have exprest
A brave and vertuous soul, but I must not
Carrie this message to her; therefore take
Your own words back agen—for, I love Cleona
With chaste and noble fire; my intents are
Fair as her brow: I dare proclaim it Sir
In my devotions, at that minute when
I know a million of adoring Spirits
Hover about the Altar.

DUKE
Do ye mock me?

FOSCARI
Pardon a truth, my Lord: I have apparrel'd
My own sense with your language.

DUKE

Do you come
To affront us? you had better ha been sleeping
In your cold Urn, as fame late gave you out,
And mingled with the rude forgotten ashes,
Than live to move our anger.

FOSCARI

Spare your frowns: it is not breath
Can fright a noble truth; nor is there Magick
I'th' person of a King.

DUKE

You threaten us.

FOSCARI

Heaven avert so black a thought;
Though in my honours cause I can be flame,
My blood is frost to treason; yet I must tell you,
I love Cleona too; and I may say
You reach not my affection: I admit
You value her above your Dukedome, health;
That you would sacrifice your blood to avert
Any mishap should threaten that dear head;
All this is but above your self: but I
Love her above her self; and while you can
But give your life, and all you have to do
Cleona service, I can give away
Her self, Cleona's self, in my love to her.
I see you are at losse; I'le reconcile
All, she is yours, this minute ends my claim;
Live, and enjoy her happilie; may you be
Famous in that beauteous Empire; She,
Blest in so great a Lord.

DUKE

I must not be
O'recome in honour; nor would do so great
A wrong to enjoy the blessing; I knew not
You were engag'd.

FOSCARI

E're you proceed, I must
Beseech you hear me out: I am but fresh
Return'd from travail; in my absence, she
Heard I was slain; at my return, upon
The hearing of these honours you intend her,
And which I now believe from your own lip,
I found a means, and have wrought her already

Into a firm belief that I am dead:
(For I have but pretended I came from her)
If for my sake you leave her now, I can
Make good her faith and die; 't sha' not be said,
I liv'd and overthrew Cleona's fortune.

DUKE
Staie miracle of honour, and of love.

FOSCARI
If you proceed, as it concerns your happiness,
I can secure all fear of me; I am
Resolv'd a course wherein I will be dead
To her, yet live to pray for her and you,
Although I never see you more: will you
My Royal Lord.

DUKE
Did ever Lover plead
Against himself before?

FOSCARI
I love her still,
And in that studie her advancement, Sir,
In you: I cannot give her.

DUKE
Well, I will still love her, and solicite.

FOSCARI
And not open that I am living.

DUKE
Not a sillable.

FOSCARI
I am confident, let me but kiss your hand
Agen: my blessings dwell with you for ever.

[Exit.

DUKE
He was alwaies noble; but this passion
Has out-gone Historie: it makes for me:
Hail to my courteous fate; Foscari thanks;
Like th' aged Phoenix thy old love expires,
And from such death springs life to my desires.

[Exit.

Foscari's Lodgings.

[Enter **DULCINO**.

DULCINO
The Father is not come yet; nor my Lord
Return'd; yet when they do, I have no way
To help my self; nor have I power to go
From hence: sure this is the Religious Man.

[Enter **VALENTIO**.

VALENTIO
Ha, 'tis the same.

DULCINO
Father Valentio?

VALENTIO
Dear Leonora?

DULCINO
Sir, the same.

VALENTIO
Oh let
My tears express my joys, what miracle
Gave you this libertie?

DULCINO
I was rescued
By th' happie valour of a Gentleman,
To whom in gratitude I pay this service:
He bid me here expect a holy man; and is it you?

VALENTIO
The circumstance confirms it.

DULCINO
Are you the good man whom my Lord expects?
'Tis some refreshing in the midst of sorrow
To meet agen.

VALENTIO
And heaven hath heard my praier.

DULCINO
But I am miserable still, unless
Your counsel do relieve me.

VALENTIO
Why my charge?

DULCINO
This noble Gentleman, to whom I owe
My preservation, who appointed you
To meet him here, having resolv'd to enter
Into Religion, hath been very urgent
For me to do so too; and overcome
With many importunities, I gave
Consent, not knowing what was best to do:
Some cure, or I am lost; you know I cannot
Mix with religious men.

VALENTIO
Did you consent?

DULCINO
I did, and he is now upon the point
Of his return.

VALENTIO
Y' are in a straight I must
Confess; no matter, hold your purpose, and
Leave all to me. He is return'd.

[Enter **FOSCARI**.

FOSCARI
Good Father,
Now I am readie; have you dispos'd him for such a life?

VALENTIO
He is constant to attend you,
I have prepat'd him, and made way to the Abbot
For your reception.

FOSCARI
I am blest, Dulcino,
Nay no distinction now, methinks we move

Upon the wings of Cherubims alreadie;
'Tis but a step to heaven; come my sweet Boy,
We climbe by a short Ladder to our joy.

[Exeunt.

SCENE IV

A Garden.

[Enter **LODWICK** and **GRIMUNDO**.

GRIMUNDO
This, my Lord, is her Garden, into which you see
My Key hath given us a private accesse.

LODWICK
'Tis full of curiositie.

GRIMUNDO
You see that Grove.

LODWICK
I do.

GRIMUNDO
There is her house of pleasure: let your eie
Entertain some delight here, while I give her happie
Knowledge you are entred.

[Exit.

LODWICK
Do so; an honest knave, I see that: how
Happie shall I be in his conversation? I sha not
Need to keep any in fee to procure, and he be
So well furnished: if ever I come to be Duke, I will
Erect a magnificent Colledge; endow it
With Revenue to maintain Wenches, and
With great Pensions invite the fairest Ladies
From all parts of Christendome into my Seraglio;
Then will I have this fellow gelded, and make him
My chief Eunuch ranger, or overseer of all
My precious tame Fowl.

[Enter **THREE SATYRS**, and lie down.

How now? what's this, some Furie asleep? Ile take another path; another? into what wilderness has this Fire-drake brought me? I dare not crie out for fear of waking 'em: would Grimundo were come back.

[Enter **SILVANUS**.

SILVANUS
Rise you drowsie Satyrs, rise;
What strong charm doth bind your eies?
See who comes into your Grove,
To embrace the Queen of Love;
Leap for joy, and frisk about,
Find your prettie Dryads out;
Hand in hand compose a ring,
Dance and circle your new King;
Him, Silvanus must obey,
Satyrs rise and run in.
Hence, and crie a holiday.

[Exit.

LODWICK
Some Mask; a device to entertain me, Ha! And yet I see not how they should prepare so much ceremony, unlesse they had expected me. A curse upon their ill faces; they shook me at first: how now?

[Enter **SATYRS** pursuing **NYMPHS**, they dance together. Exeunt **SATYRS**; **NYMPHS** seem to intreat him to go with them.

Have ye no tongues? yes I will venture my self in your company, and you were my destinies; wo'd there were no worse in hell, must I walk like a bride too, fortune set on afore then, and thou dost not guide into a hansome place, wo'd thy eyes were out, and so thou maist be taken for the blind goddess indeed; forward to Venus Temple.

[Exit.

SCENE IV

The Same. A Grove with a Banquet Prepared.

Enter **LODWICK** with the **NYMPHS** who suddenly leave him.

LODWICK
Vanished like Fayries? Ha, what musicks this? the motion of the Sphears, or am I in Elisium?

[Enter **GRIMUNDO**, bare, leading **BELINDA** richly attired, and attended by **NYMPHS**.

Here is Grimundo, Ha! what glorious creatures this commits a rape upon my sences on every side, but when I look on her, all other admirations are forgot, and lessen in her glory.

BELINDA
My Lord y'are most welcome, nay, our lip is not too precious for your salute: most welcome.

[Kisses him.

GRIMUNDO
I have kept my word Sir.

LODWICK
Thou hast oblieg'd my soul.

GRIMUNDO
Be high and frolick, she loves to see one
Domineer; when y'are throughly acquainted you'le
Give me thanks.

LODWICK
Let us be private with at much speed as may be;
Away with those gossips, so, so.

[Exeunt all but **LODWICK** and **BELINDA**.

I forgot to ask her name: Lady am come.

BELINDA
Wilt please you use that chair?

LODWICK
You are not ignorant
Of the intents my blood hath brought with me,
Grimundo I hope hath told my coming Lady.
And you I'me confident will justifie his promise
Of some pastime.

BELINDA
He's a servant,
Whose bosom I dare trust the son of night,
And yet more secret than his mother, he
Hath power to engage me, and I shall
Take pride in my obedience; first be pleas'd
To taste, what in my duty I prepar'd
For your first entertainment; these but serve
To quicken appetite.

[Recorders.

LODWICK
I like this well,
I shall not use much Courtship, where's this musick?

BELINDA
Doth it offend your ear?

LODWICK
'Tis ravishing, whence doth it breath?

BELINDA
If you command, weele change
A thousand airs, till you find one is sweet
And high enough to rock your wanton soul
Into Elisian slumbers.

LODWICK
Spare them all,
I hear 'em in thy accents.

BELINDA
Orpheus
Calliopes fam'd sonne, upon whose Lute
Myriads of lovers ghosts do wait and hang
Upon the golden strings to have their own
Griefs softned with his noble touch, shall come
Again from hell with fresh and happier strains
To move your fancy.

LODWICK
That were very strange,
She is Poetical, more than half a fury: [aside]
But we prate all this while, and lose the time
We should imploy more preciously; I need
No more provocations, my veins are rich,
And swell with expectations: shall we to
This vaulting business?

BELINDA
I shall hope my Lord
You will be silent in mine honour, when
You have enjoy'd me, and not boast my name
To your disgrace, nor mine.

LODWICK
Your name, why Lady?
By my desires I know it not: I hope

You have receiv'd a better character,
Than to suspect my blabbing: I'le not trust
My Ghostly Father with my sins, much lesse
Your name.

BELINDA
O let me flie into your arms,
These words command my freedome; I shall love
You above my self, and to confirm how much
I dare repose upon your faith, I'le not
Be nice to tell you who I am.

LODWICK
Pray do.

BELINDA
I am a Princess.

LODWICK
How?

BELINDA
Believe me sit.

LODWICK
I'm glad a that, but of what Countrey Ladie?

BELINDA
And my dominions are more spreading than
Your brothers.

LODWICK
Ha! that's excellent; if the Villain
Do prosper with my wife, I'le marrie her.

BELINDA
I was not born to perch upon a Dukedom,
Or some such spot of earth, which the dull eyes
Examine by a magnifying glass,
And wonder at; the Roman Eagles never
Did spread their wings upon so manie shores,
The silver Moon of Ottomon looks pale
Upon my great Empire; Kings of Spain,
That now may boast their ground, doth stretch as wide
As day, are but poor Landlords of a Cell,
Compar'd to mine inheritance; the truth is,
I am the Devil.

LODWICK
How a Devil?

BELINDA
Yes.
Be not affrighted Sir, you see I bring
No horror to distract you: if this presence
Delight you not, I'le wearie a thousand shapes
To please my Lord.

LODWICK
Shapes quotha.

BELINDA
Doe not tremble.

LODWICK [aside]
A Devil? I see her cloven foot: I ha not
The heart to pray, Grimundo has undone me.

BELINDA
I did command my spirits to put on
Satyrs, and Nymphs to entertain you first,
Whiles other in the aire maintain'd a quire
For your delight: why do you keep such distance
With one that loves you? Recollect your self,
You came for pleasure, what doth fright my love?
See I am covetous to return delight,
And satisfie your lustful genius:
Come let us withdraw, and on the bed prepar'd
Beget a Race of smooth and wanton Devils—

LODWICK
Hold, come not near me; Ha! now I compare
The circumstances, they induce me to
A sad belief, and I had breath enough
I would ask a question.

BELINDA
Anie thing, and be
Resolved.

LODWICK
How came Grimundo and your Devilship
Acquainted?

BELINDA
He hath been my Agent long,

And hath deserv'd for his hypocrisie,
And private sins, no common place in hell,
He's now my favourite, and we enjoy
Each other dailie; but he never did
By anie service more endear my love,
Than by this bringing you to my acquaintance,
Which I desir'd of him long since, with manie
And fierce sollicite, but he urg'd his fear,
You were not ripe enough in sin for his
Discoverie.

LODWICK
I feel my self dissolve
In sweat.

BELINDA
My Lord, I must acknowledge, I
Have ever had you in my first regard
Of anie mortal sinner, for you have
The same propention with me, though with
Less malice, spirits of the lower world
Have several offices assign'd; some are
To advance pride, some avarice, some wrath;
I am for lust, a gay voluptuous Devil,
Come lets embrace, for that I love my Lord,
Do, and command a Regiment of hell,
They all are at your service.

LODWICK
O my soul!

BELINDA
Beside my Lord, it is another motive
To honour you, and by my chains which now
I have left behind, it makes me grow enamour'd;
Your wife that sayes her prayers at home, and weeps
Away her fight; O let me hug you for it,
Despise her vows still, spurn her tears agen
Into her eyes, thou shalt be Prince in hell,
And have a Crown of flames, brighter than that
Which Ariadne wears of fixed stars;
Come shall we dallie now?

LODWICK
My bones within
Are dust alreadie, and I wear my flesh
Like a loose upper garment.

BELINDA

Y'are afraid,
Be not so pale at Liver, for I see
Your blood turns coward, how would you be frighted
To look upon me cloath'd with all my horror,
That shudder at me now? call up your spirit.

LODWICK

There are too manie spirits here alreadie,
Would thou wert conjur'd, what shall I do?

BELINDA

What other than to bathe your soul in pleasure,
And never heard of Ravishings; we two
Will progress through the aire in Venus Charriot,
And when her silver Doves grow faint and tire,
Cupid and Mercury shall lend us wings,
And we will visit new worlds when we are
Wearie of this, we both will back the winds,
And hunt the Phoenix through the Arabian Deserts,
Her we will spoil of all her shining plumes,
To make a blazing Coronet for thy Temples,
Which from the earth beheld, shall draw up wonder,
And puzzle learned Astronomie to distinguish it
From some new Constellation, the Sea
Shall yield us pastime, when inveloped
With clouds blacker than night, we range about;
And when with storms we overthrow whole Navies,
We'll laugh to hear the Mariners exclaim
In manie thousand shipwracks; what do I
Urge these particulars? let us be one soul,
Aire, earth, and hell is yours.

LODWICK

I have a suit,
But dare not speak.

BELINDA

Take courage, and from me
Be confident to obtain.

LODWICK

I am not well,
The name of Dill came too quick upon me,
I was not well prepar'd for such a sound,
It turn'd my blood to Ice, and I ha not
Recovered so much warmth yet, to desire
The sport I came for; would you please but to

Dismiss for me a time, I would return
When I have heat and strength enough for such
A sprightful action.

BELINDA
I do find your cunning,
You pretend this excuse but to gain time,
In hope you may repent.

LODWICK
And please your Grace
Not I.

BELINDA
You will acquaint some Priest or other,
A tribe of all the world I most abhor,
And they will fool you with their Ghostlie counsel,
Perplex you with some fond Divinitie,
To make you lose the glories I have promis'd.

LODWICK
I could never abide such melanchollie people.

BELINDA
In this I must betray, we spirits we have
No perfect knowledge of mens thoughts; I see
Your bloods infeebled, and although my love
Be infinite, and everie minute I
Shall languish in your absence, yet your health
I must preserve, 'tis that feeds my hopes,
Hereafter I shall perfectlie enjoy thee;
You will be faithful, and return.

LODWICK
Suspect not.

BELINDA
One kiss shall seal consent.

[Kisses him.

LODWICK
Her breath smells on brimstone.

BELINDA
For this time I'le dismiss you—do not pray,
A spirit shall attend you.

LODWICK
Do not pray? When did I last? I know not, farewell horror,
He wants a wench that goes to the Devil for her.

[Exeunt.

ACTUS V

SCENE I

A Room in Cleona's House.

Enter **ASTELLA** and **PIERO**.

ASTELLA
Touch me not Villain, pietie defend me,
Art thou a man, or have I all this while
Converst with some ill Angel in the shape
Of my Lords friend.

PIERO
What needeth all this stir,
I urge your benefit.

ASTELLA
To undo my name,
Nay soul for ever with one act.

PIERO
One act;
There be those Ladies that have acted it
A hundred times, yet think themselves as good
Christians as other women, and do carrie
As much opinion too for vertue.

ASTELLA
Heaven.

PIERO
What harm can there be in't, can you neglect
Revenge so just, so easie, and delightful?

ASTELLA
Thy breath doth scatter an infection.

PIERO

Scatter a toy, be wise, and lose no time,
You know not when such opportunitie
May tempt you to't agen; for my own part
I can but do you a pleasure in't, your blood
Should need no other argument.

ASTELLA
I'le sooner
Emptie my veins, not to redeem thy soul,
Should sin betray mine honour to one loose
Embrace: hence Traytor, I do feel corruption
I'th aire alreadie, it will kill me if
I stay: hereafter I'le not wonder how
My Lord became so wicked.

[Enter **JACOMO** behind.

PIERO
You will lead me
To some more private Room,
I'le follow Madam.

[Exeunt

JACOMO
More private Room said he? I smell a business, I thought this Gamester had been gone, is it e'ne so, have at your Burrough Madam, he's a shrewd Ferret I can tell you, and just in the nick here comes the Warrener.

[Enter **LODWICK**.

LODWICK
This Devil does not follow me, nor anie of her Cubs I hope, I'm glad I came off so well, I never was so hot to engender with the Night-mare; could Grimundo find no other creature for my coupling but a Succubus, methinks I smell the fiend still.

JACOMO
He talks on her alreadie.

LODWICK
I am verie jealous.

JACOMO
Not without a cause my Lord.

LODWICK
Ha! there she is agen.

JACOMO

No my Lord, she is new gone into the withdrawing chamber.

LODWICK

Ha! who? who is gone?

JACOMO

A Gentlewoman that you were late in companie with.

LODWICK

The Devil? look well about you then, a spirit
Of her constitution will set the house on fire
Instantlie, and make a young hell on't, when
Came she? I shall be everlastinglie haunted
With goblings, art sure thou sawest her?

JACOMO

Saw her, yes, and him too.

LODWICK

Grimundo?

JACOMO

No not Grimundo, but I saw another Gentleman
That has been held a notable spirit,
Familiar with her.

LODWICK

Spirit and familiar.

JACOMO

Piero my Lord.

LODWICK

Piero?

JACOMO

I wonot say what I think, but I think somewhat
And I know what I say, if she be a Devil, as she
Can be little less, if she be as bad as I imagine,
Some bodies head will ake for't, for mine own
Part I did but see and hear, that's all, and
Yet I ha not told you half.

LODWICK

Let me collect, sure this fellow by th' circumstance
Means Astella; thou talkest all this while of my Ladie
Doest not?

JACOMO
Yes my Lord, she is all the Ladies in the house;
For my Ladie and Mistriss was sent for
To the Abbey.

LODWICK
I had forgotten my self, this is new horror,
Is my Ladie and Piero so familiar saist, and
In private?

JACOMO
What I have said, I have said; and what they have
Done, they have done by this time.

LODWICK
Done? and I'le be active too.

JACOMO
Shew what feats of activitie you please.

[Exit **LODWICK**.

LODWICK
So so, now I am alone, which is, as
The learned say, Solus cum sola, I will entertain
Some honourable thoughts of my preferment.

[Enter **PIERO**.

Hum, the Gamester is returned; what melanchollie? then.
He has don't, I'le lay my head to a fools Cap on'c,
I was alwayes so my self after my capring.
Did you not meet the Prince sir?

PIERO
No, where is he?

JACOMO
He was here but now, and enquired how his Ladie did, and I told him you could tell the state of her
bodie better than I. for—

PIERO
I did but see her.

JACOMO
That's not the right on't, it runs for I did but kiss her, for
I did but kiss her.

PIERO
It was enough for me to kiss her hand.
I am suspected, I must turn this fools discourse
Another way, the present theam is dangerous:
What I hear say Iacomo, your Ladie is like to rise?

JACOMO
My Ladie does rise as earlie as other Ladies do that go to bed late.

PIERO
And there will be a notable preferment for you.

JACOMO
'Tis verie likelie my Ladie understands her self.

PIERO
There is a whisper abroad.

JACOMO
'Tis a good hearing.

PIERO
What if she be married in this absence?

JACOMO
Verie likelie; I say notthing, but I think I know my Ladies secrets for the triumph, as pageants, or running at tilt, you may hear more shortlie, there may be Reasons of State to have things carried privatelie, they will break out in Bells and Bonefires hereafter; what their Graces have intended for me I conceal.

PIERO [aside]
He is wound up alreadie.

JACOMO
You are a Gentleman I shall take particular notice of.

PIERO
But what if after all this imagination of a marriage, fortune should forbid the banes?

JACOMO
How? fortune's a slut, and because she is a whore her self, would have no Ladie marrie and live honest.

[Enter **LODWICK**

LODWICK
Piero, where's Piero?

PIERO

Ha my Lord I ha don't.

LODWICK
Ha, what?

PIERO
I ha pleas'd thy excellence, and you had made more haste, you might a come to the fall a'th'Deer.

LODWICK
Th'ast not enjoy'd her?

PIERO
They talk of Iupiter, and a golden shower,
Give me a Mercury with wit and tongue,
He shall charm more Ladies on their backs,
Than the whole bundle of gods pshew!

LODWICK
Shoot not so much compass, be brief and answer me; hast thou enjoy'd her?

PIERO
I have, shall I swear?

LODWICK
No, thou wilt be damn'd sufficientlie without an oath; in the mean time I do mean to reward your nimble diligence: draw.

PIERO
What dee mean?

JACOMO
And you be so sharp-set I do mean to withdraw.

[Exit.

LODWICK
I do mean to cut your throat, or perish i'th attempt, you see your destinie, my birth and spirit wo'not let me kill thee in the dark; draw, and be circumspect.

PIERO
Did not you engage me to it? have I done anie thing but by your directions? my Lord.

LODWICK
'Tis all one, my mind is altered, I will see what complexion your heart bears; if I hit upon the right vein, I may cure your disease a'th blood.

PIERO

Hold, and there be no remedie, I will die better than I ha liv'd; you shall see sir that I dare fight with you, and if I fall by your sword, my base consent to act your will deserves it.

[Draws.

LODWICK
Ha!

PIERO
I find your policie, and by this storm
You'd prove my Resolution, how boldlie I
Dare stand to't when this great
Dishonour comes to question, prepare
To be displeased—she is a miracle
Of Chastitie, impenetrable like
A marble, she returned my sinful arrows,
And they have wounded me; forgive me Ladie.

LODWICK
I prethee tell me true; now thou shalt swear,
Hast thou not don't.

PIERO
Not by my hope of heaven
Which I had almost forfeited, had not she
Relieved me with her vertue; in this truth
I dare resign my breath.

LODWICK
I dare believe thee:
What did I see in her to doubt her firmness?

[Enter **JACOMO** and **ASTELLA**.

JACOMO
Here they are Madam, you do not mean to
Run upon their weapons.

LODWICK
Piero thou shalt wonder.

ASTELLA
What means my Lord?

LODWICK
You shall know that anon;
My Ladie go with me.

ASTELLA
Whither you please,
You shall not need to force me sir, you may
Lead me with gossamere, or the least thread
The industrious Spider weaves.

[Exeunt **LODWICK** and **ASTELLA**.

JACOMO
Whimsies.

PIERO
What furie thus transport him at some distance,
I'le follow him, he may intend some violence,
She is too good to suffer, I shall grow
In love with my conversion.

[Exit.

JACOMO
Grow in love with a Cockscomb, his last words
Stick on my stomack still fortune forbid the bans
Quotha slid if fortune, should forbid the banes,
And my Ladie be not converted into a Dutchess
Where are all my offices?
Hum! Where are they, quoth I? I do not know;
But of all tunes I shall hate Fortune my foe.

[Exit.

SCENE II

An Abbey. The Abbot's Lodgings.

[Recorders, Chairs prepared. Enter **SORANZO, GIOTTO**.

SORANZO
Know you not who they are my Lord this day
Receive the habit?

GIOTTO
I can meet with no intelligence.

SORANZO
They are persons of some qualitie—

GIOTTO
The Duke does mean to grace their Ceremonie.

SORANZO
He was invited by the Abbot to their cloathing.

GIOTTO
Which must be in private too, here in his lodgings.

SORANZO
Well we shall not long expect 'em, his Grace enters.

[Enter **DUKE, GRIMUNDO**.

GRIMUNDO
It helpt much that he never saw my wife.

DUKE
Dost think 'twill take?

GRIMUNDO
There's some hope my Lord alreadie,
And heaven may prosper it.

DUKE
We cannot endear thee to thy merit.

SORANZO
How the Duke embraces him.

[Enter **CLEONA**, attended.

DUKE
Cleona you are welcom, 'tis a blest
Occasion that makes us meet so happilie.

CLEONA
It pleas'd my Lord Abbot to invite me hither.

DUKE
I appear'd too upon his friendlie summons,
We'll thank him for this presence.

SORANZO
The Abbot enters.

[Enter the **ABBOT**, attended with **RELIGIOUS MEN**, having bowed to the **DUKE**, he taketh a Chair; being sate, **VALENTIO** goes out, and presently enters, leading **FOSCARI** and **DULCINO** in St. Bennets habit, he presents them, they kneel at the Abbots feet.

ABBOT
Speak your desire.

FOSCARI
We kneel to be received into the number
Of those Religious men that dedicate
Themselves to heaven i'th'habit of St. Bennet,
And humblie pray that you would rectifie
And teach our weak devotion the way
To imitate his life, by giving us
The precepts of your order.

ABBOT
Let me tell you,
You must take heed the ground of your Resolve
Be perfect; yet look back into the spring
Of your desires, Religious men should be
Tapers, first lighted by a holie beam:
Meteors may shine like stars, but are not constant.

FOSCARI
We covet not the blaze, which a corrupt
And slimie matter may advance, our thoughts
Are flam'd with charitie.

ABBOT
Yet ere you embark,
Think on your hard adventure, there is more
To be examin'd beside your end,
And the Reward of such an undertaking;
You look on heaven afar off, like a land-skip,
Whether wild thoughts like your imperfect eye,
Without examination of those wayes,
Oblique and narrow are transported, but
I'th walk and tryal of the difficulties
That interpose, you tire like inconsiderate
And wearie Pilgrims.

FOSCARI
We desire to know
The Rules of our obedience.

ABBOT
They will startle

Your Resolutions; can your will, not us'd
To anie Law beside it self, permit
The knowledge of severe and positive limits?
Submit to be controul'd, imploy'd sometime
In servile offices, against the greatness
Of your high birth and sufferance of nature?
Can you, forgetting all youthful desire,
And memorie of the worlds betraying pleasures,
Check wanton heat, and consecrate your blood
To Chastitie, and holie solitude?

SORANZO
I wonot be Religious Giotto.

GIOTTO
Nor I, upon these terms, I pitie em.

ABBOT
Can you quit all the glories of your state,
Resign your titles and large wealth, to live
Poor and neglected, change high food and surfets
For a continual fasting, your down-beds
For hard and humble lodging, your gilt Roofs
And Galleries for a melanchollie Cell,
The pattern of agrave, where, stead of musick
To charm you into slumbers, to be wak'd
With the sad chiming of the sacring Bell;
Your Robes, whose curiositie hath tyred
Invention, and the Silk-worm to adorn you,
Your blaze of Jewels, that your pride have worn
To burn out Envies eyes, must be no more
Your ornament, but coarse, and rugged cloathing
Harrow your skins; these, and manie more
Unkind austerities will much offend
Your tender constitutions; yet consider.

DUKE
He does insist much on their state and honour:
May we not know em yet?

VALENTIO
One of them sir
Doth owe this character.

[Gives him a paper.

DUKE
It is Foscari,

I find his noble purpose, he is perfect:
I honour thee young man, she must not see
This paper.

[Gives another paper.

VALENTIO
This doth speak the other Sir.

DUKE
'Tis at large—ha—Grimundo, I prithee read,
I dare not credit my own eyes: Leonora,
So it begins, Leonora.

GRIMUNDO
Leonora, Daughter to the late Gonzaga, Duke
Of Millan, fearing she should be compelled to marry
Her Uncle, in the habit of a Page, and the conduct
Of Father Valentio, came to Savoy, to try the
Love and honour of his Excellence, who once
Solicited by his Embassador—

DUKE
No more, I am extasied;
If so much blessing may be met at once,
Ile do my heart that justice to proclaim
Thou hadst a deep impression; as a boy
I lov'd thee too, for It could be no other,
But with a Divine flame; fair Leonora,
Like to a perfect magnes, though inclos'd
With an Ivorie box, through the white wall
Shot forth imbracing vertue: now, oh now
Our Destinies are kind.

[Embraces her.

FOSCARI
This is a misterie, Dulcino?

CLEONA
No my Lord, I am discovered;
You see Leonora now, a Millan Ladie,
If I may hope your pardon—

DUKE
Love and honour
Thou dost enrich my heart: Cleona read,
And entertain the happiness to which

Thy Fate predestin'd thee, whilst I obey
Mine here.

[Gives **CLEONA** the letter.

[**CLEONA** reads.

CLEONA
How, my Lord Foscari?
If he be living, I must die before
This separation be confirm'd; my joy
Doth overcome my wonder; can you leave
The world, while I am in't?

FOSCARI
Dear'st Leonora!
Then willinglie I dispence with my intention,
And if the Duke have found another Mistris,
It shall be my devotion to pray here,
And my Religion to honour thee.

ABBOT
Manie blessings crown this union.

FOSCARI
Your pardon gracious Princesse,
I did impose too much.

CLEONA
I studied
To be your grateful Servant, as your self
Unto the fair Cleona; we are all happie.

[Enter **LODWICK, ASTELLA,** and **PIERO**.

LODWICK
They're here; by your leave Brother, my Lord Abbot,

[Kneels to him.

Witness enough.

DUKE
Why thus kneels Lodwick?

LODWICK
To make confession Brother, and beg heavens,
And everie good mans pardon, for the wrong

I ha done this excellent Ladie, whom my soul
New marries, and may heaven—ha, do not hold
A justice back: Grimundo is a traitor,
Take heed on him, and say your praiers; he is
The Devils grand Solicitor for souls.
He hath not such another cunning engine i'th
World to ruine vertue.

GRIMUNDO
I, my Lord?

LODWICK
You are no hypocrite: he does everie night
Lie with a Succubus; he brought me to one,
Let him denie it; but heaven had pittie on me.

[Enter **BELINDA**., disguised as before, and kneels to the **DUKE**.

Ha! there she is: do you not see her? Devil
I do defie thee: my Lord, stand by me:
I will be honest spight of him and thee,
And lie with my own Wife.

GIOTTO
Sure the Prince is mad.

DUKE
O rise most noble Ladie, well deserving
A statue to record thy vertue.

LODWICK
Ha!

DUKE
This is Grimundo's Wife.

LODWICK
'Tis so, my Lord.

BELINDA
No Devil, but the servant of your vertue,
That shall rejoice if we have thriv'd in your conversion.

ASTELLA
I hope it.

LODWICK
Have I bin mockt into honestie?

Are not you a Furie? and you a slie and subtile Epicure?

GRIMUNDO
I do abhor the thought of being so:
Pardon my seeming, Sir.

ABBOT
O go not back,
Prevent thus seasonable your real torment.

LODWICK
I am fullie wakened, be this kisse the Pledge
Of my new heart.

PIERO
True love stream in your bosomes;
Ladie forgive me too.

ASTELLA
Most willinglie.

DUKE
Our joy is perfect: Lodwick salute
A Sifter in this Ladie Leonora,
The object of our first love; take the story
As we return: Lord Abbot we must thank
You for contriving this; and you good Father.
Embassadors shall be dispatcht to Millan,
To acquaint 'em where, and how their absent Princess
Leonora hath dispos'd her self; meanwhile,
Poets shall stretch invention, to express
Triumphs for thee, and Savoys happiness.

[Exeunt **OMNES**.

JAMES SHIRLEY – A CONCISE BIBLIOGRAPHY

The following includes years of first publication, and of performance if known, together with dates of licensing by the Master of the Revels if available.

TRAGEDIES
The Maid's Revenge (licensed 9th February 1626; printed, 1639)
The Traitor (licensed 4th May 1631; printed, 1635)
Love's Cruelty (licensed 14th November 1631; printed, 1640)
The Politician (acted, 1639; printed, 1655)
The Cardinal (licensed 25th May 1641; printed, 1652).

www.ingramcontent.com/pod-product-compliance
Lightning Source LLC
Chambersburg PA
CBHW060133050426
42448CB00010B/2098